Twayne's United States Authors Series

Sylvia E. Bowman, *Editor*

INDIANA UNIVERSITY

Frank Norris

FRANK NORRIS

by WARREN FRENCH

TWAYNE PUBLISHERS
A DIVISION OF G. K. HALL & CO., BOSTON

Library of Congress Catalog Card Number: 62-16820

ISBN 0-8057-0552-X

MANUFACTURED IN THE UNITED STATES OF AMERICA

FOR
MARC
WHO VINDICATED
MY FAITH IN
TEACHING

Contents

Chapter

	Chronology	15
1.	Pride of Fiji	19
2.	March We Must	35
3.	Young Man's Fancy	49
4.	The Gilded Cage	62
5.	Victorian Valkyries	76
6.	A Large Enough View	89
7.	"It's When You Are Quiet That You Are at Your Best"	107
8.	Stubble	119
9.	Cricket Chorus	127
	Notes and References	142
	Selected Bibliography	148
	Index	155

Preface

POSTERITY has served Frank Norris well. Few American authors have had their remains handled with such loving care as the exuberant Californian who died at thirty-two, his most ambitious project uncompleted.

His works have been enthusiastically if uncritically preserved in a collected edition. He is the subject of an able biography and an exhaustive analysis of the influences upon his writing. His letters have been tastefully edited, and his literary remains made the subject of a nation-wide search by the University of California library. His most memorable works are in print in reasonably priced editions, while many of his contemporaries languish. He is almost always mentioned respectfully—occasionally affectionately—by historians of American literature as a drum major of the native naturalistic movement.

Despite all this attention—including a recent revival of interest that has produced intelligent revaluations that enable us to see his work in new perspectives—Norris has not been recognized for what he principally is. The very stressing of his relationship to the naturalistic movement has been an understandable misfortune—not only because it led to his temporary eclipse after World War II when naturalism went out of fashion, but also because it has obscured the most distinctive characteristic of his works.

Norris is actually best described not by one of the many writers about his works, but by John Berryman's offhand remark in *Stephen Crane* that Norris was "a romantic moralist, with a style like a great wet dog." Many critics—especially those influenced by Granville Hicks's *The Great Tradition* (1933)— have pounced upon inconsistencies in Norris' thinking and allegedly naturalistic writing that they have supposed adequate to deny his claim to fame. What such critics fail to realize is that rigorous scientific consistency would be utterly alien to Norris' dramatic, dynamic personality, and that his closest link is not with the imported naturalistic tradition but with the transcendentalist tradition of those native writers who most vigorously denounced consistency—Emerson and Whitman.

The most useful clue to understanding Norris' work is provided by Alfred Kazin's passing remark in *On Native Grounds* (1942) that *The Pit* "proved no more than that the hold of the pit over Curtis Jadwin was exactly like the hold of drink over the good but erring father in a temperance novel." Kazin does not go on to observe, however, that the similarity he notes is by no means limited in Norris' work to the portrayal of Jadwin. All of the author's novels resemble temperance tracts.

Richard Chase comments in *The American Novel and Its Tradition* (1957) that Norris employs "the conspiracy theory of history"—the idea that man's ills can all be traced back to some single specific evil (not just the "money power" that Chase cites, but alcohol, slavery, bleached flour, bathing, etc.) that has always been the mainstay of the panacea-seeking tractarian. Like most romantic thinkers, Norris is essentially one who seeks to reform not specific institutions, but human nature; and the vehicle of moral reform is the tract, one of the bulkiest if least admired pillars of the American literary tradition.

The reasons for the original classification of Norris as a naturalist are apparent. Early readers and critics, distressed by the violence of Norris' best received books, *McTeague* and *The Octopus,* had to seek a theoretical justification for works they found literally distasteful. As late as 1915 such a conservative spokesman as Fred Lewis Pattee was writing in *American Literature since 1870* that Norris was "an ardent disciple of Zola," who swung to the extreme of the French author's theories, as if "to tell the truth was to tell with microscopic details the repulsive things of physical life."

Although the attitude Pattee represents persists at least as late as 1951 when Arthur Hobson Quinn's *The Literature of the American People* appeared, few today need to call upon experimental naturalism to excuse Norris. We have become calloused against far grosser events and language than he employed. Since those who have maintained that Norris is not a consistent naturalist are quite right (the second chapter of this book describes the philosophy actually underlying his work), we must find another justification for considering his work worth attention.

My argument is that this justification is found in Norris' preserving almost unadulterated in an age characterized by the pessimism and cynicism of Mark Twain, Stephen Crane, and Ambrose Bierce, a transcendentalist romantic faith in the grand design of a benevolent "Nature" epitomized in the story of the shepherd Vanamee in *The Octopus*. There is defeat and tragedy in Norris' work; but his characters suffer not because—like Stephen Crane's—they are victims of an indifferent universe but because of their selfish efforts to thwart Nature's benevolent intentions.

Norris was unquestionably profoundly influenced by the naturalists, especially Zola. How much he owes to the French author—perhaps even in the way of incidents as well as techniques—has been established by Lars Åhnebrink's exhaustive monographs. Yet Norris himself did little to advance the efforts of the naturalists. He nowhere gives evidence of being much interested in naturalistic devices except as a means to tractarian ends. Far from being a "literary scientist," he probably found much of Zola's theorizing incomprehensible. What Norris realized was that naturalism had provided him with a tool for refurbishing the nearly moribund tractarian tradition. The endless repetition of nineteenth-century tracts and the squeamishness of genteel "parlor reformers" had driven bored readers to continental fiction or to the despised dime novels for literary excitement. Imitating the naturalists might, however, make tracts as thrilling as dime novels. Charles Walcutt calls Norris' naturalism a "mannerism," but it was more than that—like the ingenious devices advertisers resort to today when sales languish, it was a technique to revive dwindling interest. Norris owes more to naturalism than it does to him. This scientific and objective literary doctrine provided techniques to give new vigor to what is best described as Norris' "romantic anarchism," the intuitive and subjective belief that a beneficent "Nature" will prevail despite the organized efforts of selfish men.

Norris' work remains valuable because the kind of "romantic anarchism" which his thinking illustrates still persists—as is indicated by the incessant cries today for "natural rights" without "civilized responsibilities." I propose, therefore, to write of Norris not as a historical landmark or a museum piece, but as one manifestation of a persisting American state of mind—not as an American convert to a foreign literary tradition, but as a scion of the transcendentalists who, with proverbial Yankee ingenuity, borrowed the latest techniques to give new impetus to the irrepressible tradition of American romanticism.

WARREN FRENCH

Cornish Flat, New Hampshire

Acknowledgments

For permission to quote from the works of Frank Norris in the Collected Edition of 1928 as well as from the introductions to the volumes of that edition I am greatly indebted to Doubleday and Company, Inc., who have also kindly granted permission to quote from *Frank Norris, A Biography* by Franklin Walker (copyright 1932 by the author) and *The American Novel and Its Tradition* by Richard Chase (copyright 1957 by the author). Quotations from *The Letters of Frank Norris*, edited by Franklin Walker (copyright 1956), appear through the courtesy of the publisher, the Book Club of California.

I wish also to thank Harcourt, Brace & World, Inc., for permission to reprint from S. I. Hayakawa's *Language in Thought and Action*; Harper and Brothers, for permission to quote from *An American Visitor* by Joyce Cary; and the Viking Press, Inc., for permission to use material from John Steinbeck's *The Grapes of Wrath*.

Quotations from H. Willard Reninger's "Norris Explains *The Octopus*" and George Meyer's "A New Interpretation of *The Octopus*" appear through the courtesy of the editors of *American Literature* and *College English* respectively, in which these articles first appeared.

That this book has been written is a tribute to the enthusiasm and encouragement of the general editor of this series, Sylvia Bowman. I owe special thanks also to Robert J. Griffin for serving as my agent in Berkeley.

Chronology

1870   March 5, Benjamin Franklin Norris, Jr., born in Chicago.

1871   October 8-9, Norris' father's place of business destroyed in Chicago fire.

1878   Norris family takes the "grand tour" of Europe and winters in Brighton, England.

1881   Frank's novelist brother, Charles Gilman Norris, born.

1882   Norris family occupies mansion on Michigan Avenue at Park Row.

1884   Family moves to Lake Merritt on the outskirts of Oakland, California.

1885   Family moves into Henry Scott mansion at 1822 Sacramento Street, San Francisco. Frank sent to a boy's preparatory school at Belmont, California.

1886   Frank attends Boys' High School, San Francisco; then the San Francisco Art Association.

1887   Family goes to Paris; Frank enrolls in the Bouguereau Studio of the Julien Atelier to study painting.

1889   Frank abandons art study in Paris and returns home; publishes his first article, "Clothes of Steel" in the San Francisco *Chronicle*.

1890   Frank enters the University of California at Berkeley as a student of limited status.

1891   Mrs. Norris subsidizes publication of *Yvernelle;* Frank joins Phi Gamma Delta.

1894   Parents divorced; Frank moves with mother and brother Charles to Harvard to study creative writing under Lewis Gates.

1895   Frank goes to Africa; becomes involved in Jameson Raid on Johannesburg.

1896   Frank develops tropical fever and is expelled from Transvaal; recuperates at Big Dipper Mine, Colfax, California;

in April becomes sub-editor of the *Wave*; meets Bruce Porter and Jeannette Black.

1897 Depressed, Frank takes leave from the *Wave* and returns to the Big Dipper Mine to complete *McTeague*; meets Captain Joseph Hodgson.

1898 *Moran of the Lady Letty* published in the Wave; Frank moves to New York City to write for *McClure's Magazine*; meets William Dean Howells; Goes to Cuban theatre of Spanish-American War as correspondent; meets Stephen Crane, Richard Harding Davis, and Frederic Remington; contracts malaria and returns to San Francisco to recuperate; *Moran of the Lady Letty* published in October.

1899 *McTeague* published in February; *Blix* published; Norris returns to California to collect material for *The Octopus*; becomes reader for Doubleday, Page and Company.

1900 January 12, Marries Jeannette Black; responsible for publication of Dreiser's *Sister Carrie*; *A Man's Woman* published; *The Octopus* completed on December 15.

1901 Frank and Jeannette go to Chicago to collect material for *The Pit*.

1902 February 9, Jeannette Norris, Jr., born; Norrises move to San Francisco and plan tramp steamer trip around the world; Jeannette has appendicitis operation; Frank dies on October 25 of perforated appendix and peritonitis.

* * * * * * *

1903 *The Pit* published after serialization in *Saturday Evening Post; A Deal in Wheat and Other Stories* and *The Responsibilities of a Novelist* published.

1904 William A. Brady produces Channing Pollock's dramatization of *The Pit*.

1909 *The Third Circle* (short stories) published.

1914 *Vandover and the Brute* edited by Charles Norris and published.

1924 Erich Von Stroheim films *McTeague* under the title *Greed*.

1932 Collected edition of Norris' work.

1956 Norris' letters edited and published.

Frank Norris

CHAPTER 1

Pride of Fiji

I   *Fastidious Bohemian*

A STAINED-GLASS WINDOW in the Phi Gamma Delta chapter house at the University of California commemorates the mercurial Frank Norris, who spent some of his happiest days as a brother of this social fraternity whose members are widely known as "Fijis." Few American writers have been enthusiastic fraternity men—it is hard to imagine Melville or James or Faulkner even "wearing the pin." Fewer still would have been likely to lend their name to an annual dinner celebrated by each chapter, but it is fortunate that at least this one outstanding writer has. Participation in a college social fraternity has for more than a century been a principal distinguishing mark of an influential group in American society, and American literature would be poorer if the voice of this group were not heard outside its cloister.

What the social fraternity does for its members is rarely understood by self-appointed critics or the members themselves. Upon arriving at college, freshmen are expected to think responsibly for the first time in their lives. Many fall by the wayside simply from paralysis occasioned by the shock of the unprecedented demand. The fraternity accepts the individual apparently as he is and thus offers a refuge where he may maintain his dignity without developing his mind.

College chums recall that Norris was happier in the chapter house than in the classroom and that he defended the often criticized physical "hazing" of pledges. Since Norris was stubbornly satisfied with his ideas and—as we shall see in an examination of his philosophy—favored only technical education, he would have resented efforts to challenge or change his thinking. Participating in fraternity hazing afforded him—as it has many others—an unconscious anti-intellectual compensation for the "intellectual hazing" he had to endure in the classroom.

The "Greek" attitude of inherent superiority colors much of Norris' work. He was probably not even aware of much of the racial and class snobbery in his writing. His denunciation of the activities of society women reflects disgusted conversation of the overgrown boys at the chapter house. The assignment of mannish names and characteristics to his heroines may simply reflect the association in his mind between the idea of people living happily together and the fraternity. His embarrassment when talking about his work and the perplexing descents into baby-talk in his letters could also have been conditioned by the Phi Gams' friendly but persistent ribbing of self-centered youngsters who talked too long or pompously about themselves. Norris himself wrote that "the regular fellow," " 'joshes' about everything and everybody and never talks about himself."[1]

The worst thing about the fraternity attitude is that it may persist long after members graduate, as it does in Norris' writings. Despite their superficial array of officials and rituals, fraternities are anarchical. The group functions to reinforce the members' assumption that they are really right when they insist—as Norris does in his essays—that the school may teach a few technical tricks but has no effect upon the thinking or personality of the individual. The fraternity reassures man of his natural goodness.

Although Frank Norris attended the University of California for four years, he never received a degree. He was never even accepted as a regular student. When he went to Harvard, he studied only creative writing and French (which he found easy). He was an indifferent student—willing to study only what he already knew.[2] Even his dislike of ROTC was more likely the result of a distaste for discipline than of anti-militarism, since he was quite enamored of fencing and brawling while an undergraduate.

He was, however, an enthusiastic participant in fraternity pranks and "functions" as empty as the women's affairs he condemned. After joining the "Fijis" on June 10, 1891, he became for three years a resident of the double gabled house on Dana Street in a room whose walls were covered with souvenirs of his stay in Paris. Not until late in his life when he came to write *The Pit* did he feel the urge to learn anything that did not "come naturally" to him, and his wife reports that never before had he been so despondent about his writing.[3] As Charles Kaplan shows, Norris, when he needed technical details for

McTeague, simply cribbed them as he had his Latin assignments.[4]
Throughout his life Norris advocated *doing* and *feeling* over
thinking, and in both novels and essays he condemned any but
technical training in college.[5] Both of these opinions must have
been the result of his own experience with unsympathetic instructors and show that, with the support of the "Fijis," he was
willing to accept himself as a model for the universe.

He could hardly have formed such a favorable picture without
the kind of support a fraternity affords, for his preoccupations in
his early novels, *Vandover and the Brute* and *McTeague,* show
that he must have been afflicted with terrifying self-doubts.
Even his failure as a student probably troubled him greatly—
despite his self-indulgent unwillingness to do anything to improve his standing—for his almost sadistic satirization, through
the multi-degreed Annixter in *The Octopus,* of the lack of preparation for the problems of life that college affords has the
marks of a remarkable piece of rationalization. Norris would
surely have been totally estranged from his college and would
not have returned to a football game as a loyal alumnus a few
days before his death if he had not found something there
which he valued as much as he despised the classroom.

He must have been especially concerned about being "accepted" at college since he was no stranger to failure when he
enrolled. He had already felt obliged to abandon the great
ambition of his youth—to become a painter—apparently from
lack of either talent or persistence. His trouble was surely not
want of funds; these were abundantly supplied by his *nouveau
riche* family.

Norris' father had been born on a Michigan farm, but was
unfitted for rural life by a chronic hip ailment. Instead of going
to school, he apprenticed himself to a jeweler and rose in time
to be head of a large wholesale jewelry business in Chicago. Like
Curtis Jadwin in *The Pit,* he was that characteristic phenomenon
of the post-Civil War United States—a self-made man.

He supplied the household with money; his wife—in accord
with the Victorian sense of the proprieties—supplied the culture.
Daughter of a New England farmer, descended from a line of
Unitarian ministers, and one of his pupils at a seminary at
Charlestown, West Virginia, she had given up school-teaching to
go on the stage, and the stage to become a grand lady in the
manner of Laura Jadwin. To display her histrionic abilities

after marrying she read Scott and Dickens aloud to her children. Benjamin Franklin, Jr., the first of five children to survive infancy, was born in 1870, the year before the great Chicago fire. Older and younger sisters died soon after birth, and Frank was the only child in the household until his brother Lester was born in 1878. His youngest brother Charles followed in 1881.

The year after Charles was born—when Frank was twelve— the family moved into a mansion on Michigan Avenue at Park Row, but did not remain there long. Troubled by Chicago's climate, the elder Norris moved to Oakland, California, in 1884, and the next year into San Francisco. There, after a period in the Palace Hotel, he purchased for the then impressive price of ten thousand dollars the Henry Scott house on Sacramento Street, two blocks from the Polk Street shopping district that was to provide the setting for *McTeague*. Once established among the opulent young city's leading citizens, Mr. Norris dabbled in building cheap houses like the father in *Vandover and the Brute,* and taught Sunday School like Jadwin in *The Pit.* Mrs. Norris became a leading light in the Browning Society.

American literature has benefited from the luxurious life Norris knew as a child. His inside knowledge of the leisure class immortalized by Veblen as the symbol of America during the Gilded Age, made it possible for him to escape the effects of the kind of impoverished childhood suffered by many "realistic" and "naturalistic" novelists who could not speak without envy or rancor of conditions Norris took for granted. While many writers have studied this Society, few have been able to give an intimate insight into the raw, unsophisticated ruthlessness that motivated "conspicuous consumption."

Norris was never a good scholar, although he would spend hours mastering the technical details of a subject that caught his fancy. He was sent to an exclusive preparatory school at Belmont, founded by William T. Reed, former president of the University of California, but he was more interested in playing with lead soldiers and making up tales about them than in mastering the arid traditional curriculum. After breaking an arm playing football, Frank dropped out of this school that specialized in intensive preparation for college.

When his arm healed, his father reputedly insisted that he try preparing for a business career at Boys' High School; but when he didn't like it there, he was allowed to enter the San

Francisco Art Association instead. He was not—as the myth of
the self-made man might make us suppose—disinherited for
taking up painting. Instead—of all the unlikely persons—George
C. Stebbins, choir-master of the great revivalist Dwight L.
Moody, who was the elder Norris' personal friend, encouraged
the family to take Frank to London for professional training.
Mr. Norris even left behind his extensive business interests to
accompany his medieval-minded son abroad. At first only the
two were supposed to go, but when Norris' brother Lester died
suddenly of diphtheria in June, 1887, Mrs. Norris and Charles
joined the party.

The London schools not satisfying them, the Norrises pro-
ceeded to Paris, where Frank was enrolled at the fashionable
Bouguereau studio of the Julien Atelier (Bouguereau is often
mentioned in Norris' work as an example of an "outdated"
master.) Frank also went with his mother to study in Florence
and Rome. His painting, however, languished when he took
up fencing and became an opera buff. Then he became infatuated with Froissart's *Chronicles* and developed into an
expert on medieval armor. Left alone by his family at eighteen,
he began to spend more time with the pen than the brush.
His interest in armor led to his first publication, "Clothes of
Steel," an anonymous article in the San Francisco *Chronicle*,
March 31, 1889. He also began entertaining his brother Charles
with installments from the unlikely history of a character named
Robert d'Artois, who had grown from a Gaston le Fox, around
whom the boys had built tales while playing with lead soldiers.
Although the naturalists were then at the peak of their influence
in France and Zola's *La Terre* appeared during Norris' stay in
Paris, he was impervious to them.

The usual story is that when Norris' father discovered what
his son was doing, he insisted, in the stereotyped manner of the
outraged Victorian parent, upon the boy's returning home immediately. A more likely version, in view of Norris' usually
getting his own way from early childhood, is that of Ernest
Peixotto, a close associate of Frank's in both San Francisco and
Paris, who says that the young man grew discouraged with his
monumental painting of the Battle of Crecy, gave the huge
canvas for it to Peixotto and another friend, Guy Rose, and
decided to go home.

Back in America Norris entered the University of California, although a deficiency in mathematics entitled him only to limited status. This young man whom a college friend describes as then "tall, gaunt, sallow-complexioned . . . yet strikingly handsome"[6] may have gone to Berkeley to prepare to enter his father's business, but he failed to take a program that would have suited this end. He concentrated on English, although he did not like the instructors, and on French. He continued to write medieval tales and poems for campus and city publications, even after Ralph Hathorn introduced him into Phi Gamma Delta, and while he was a sophomore his mother advanced four hundred dollars to Lippincott's to publish his long ballad *Yvernelle* in a lavishly illustrated holiday edition. Nothing except the hazy reminiscences of Charles Norris—who was only nine when Frank entered college—indicates that the family ever supposed Frank would not follow some kind of artistic calling. In a petition to the Academic Senate of the university to change his status to that of a special student ineligible for a degree, Norris himself wrote, "I entered college with the view of preparing myself for the profession of a writer of fiction."[7]

Norris apparently "discovered" Zola while studying French at Berkeley. Although he had ignored the great experimental writers and painters while in Paris, be began to carry yellow paper-bound novels around with him and to expound the virtues of naturalism, which there is little evidence he understood. He was probably quite ready to abandon the Middle Ages for the world of the 1890's anyway, for out of class he was having a good time. He wrote for a short-lived campus humor magazine, *Smiles,* and for the school annual. He wrote the Junior Class farce and participated in college theatricals. He is also credited with originating the plotting of football plays for the newspapers,[8] and he enjoyed playing poker and drinking at Hagerty's Saloon with the campus merrymakers.

Channing Pollock even reports that Norris fell in love with a prostitute to whom his fellow students introduced him without identifying her profession, and that he wrote verses to her.[9] This tale has been told of so many collegians that it is probably apocryphal. Norris himself wrote a short story, "The Way of the World," about such an affair, but this could have been either the cause or the effect of the story circulated about him. That such tales are told of him is, however, evidence of the kind of pompously naïve undergraduate he must have been.

While Norris was still a student, he received another blow—the divorce of his parents—that, coming on top of the failure of his career as a painter and his academic difficulties, must have seriously disturbed him and stirred up doubts about the self-indulgent life he was leading. In 1892, the elder Norris left alone on a trip around the world and, upon returning, filed suit in Chicago against his wife. Mrs. Norris filed a countersuit and obtained a decree in 1894. Mr. Norris remarried and upon his death in 1900 bestowed his whole fortune—estimated at a million dollars—on his second wife. While there is no evidence that Frank was greatly disturbed about the loss of either father or money, the breakup of the marriage must have shocked his sensibilities deeply in an age when divorce was still a scandal. Even in his last novel, *The Pit,* Norris was still pondering the problem of how to prevent a marriage from collapsing.

When Frank's four-year stay at the university finally came to nothing, his mother, who had reportedly been unwilling to give up her social life to travel with his father, packed up and moved with her son across the continent to Harvard. There, in the classroom of Lewis E. Gates, Frank at last found the inspiration that the Berkeley English department had not provided. For Gates, Norris wrote as weekly compositions large sections of his two—earliest novels; and one piece, finally incorporated into *Vandover and the Brute,* appeared in the Harvard *Advocate* as "The End of the Act." Norris also read more Zola and also George Eliot, a writer who may have had more influence than has been acknowledged in keeping alive the young author's moralizing tendencies.

Possibly to escape his family altogether, but more probably to accumulate "story material," Norris decided in 1895 to make a trip across Africa from Cape Town to Cairo. The San Francisco *Chronicle* was to publish his reports. He got to Africa, but not very far into it. After dispatching a few accounts of local entertainment and the mining industry, he became involved in the Jameson Raid, one of the episodes that led to the Boer War, and caught a severe case of South African fever, the first of his serious health difficulties.

When he recovered, the enraged Boers, who then controlled the Transvaal, gave him twenty-four hours to leave the country, which he did in a weakened condition, traveling back to England on the same ship that carried Cecil Rhodes home after the

Jameson fiasco. Returning to San Francisco, Norris spent six weeks recuperating and then took his first real job at twenty-five dollars a week.

He became assistant to the editor of the San Francisco *Wave*, a paper founded to publicize the elaborate "Del Monte," a resort hotel near Monterey. Under John O'Hara Cosgrave's editorship, the weekly had become the mouthpiece of Collis Huntington, president of the Southern Pacific Railroad and the model for Shelgrim in *The Octopus*; but it served also as an outlet for the major regional writers. Under his own name and the pseudonym of Justin Sturgis, Norris made about one hundred identifiable contributions to the magazine in less than two years—between April, 1896 and January, 1898. He even conducted a weekly column analyzing football games. Although most of the writing is ephemeral, the *Wave* gave Norris practice in solving two of the young writer's most troublesome problems—finding material and meeting deadlines.

Since he never earned more than a hundred dollars a month in this pleasant and useful but hardly rigorous job, and since he was again living a kind of posh bohemian life with friends from Phi Gam and Gelett Burgess' set, Norris was at twenty-seven still financially dependent on his mother. If *Blix* is at all autobiographical, he was also gambling and worrying again about his self-indulgence. The gay life he led was probably an escape from feelings of extreme depression, for during this period he wrote "The Puppets and the Puppy," his most cynical work. His own state of mind is probably summed up in the sketch he published in the *Wave* (May 16, 1896) about a Western City "Art Student":

> He has given his life to his work. He grows older; he tries to make his "art" pay. He drifts into decorative art; is employed perhaps as a clerk in an art store. If he's lucky he is taken on a newspaper and does the pen-and-ink work that he once affected to despise. He's over thirty by this time, and is what he will be for the rest of his life. All his ambitions are vanished, his enthusiasm's dead, but little by little he comes to be quite content.[10]

Norris himself might have continued gadding about, pilfering his manuscripts to meet deadlines and rationalizing away fits of depression by telling himself that he, too, would become contented with his inconspicuous lot, if he had not met Jeannette Black and Captain Joseph Hodgson. Miss Black, the seventeen-year-old daughter of an Irish-born forty-niner, is the original of *Blix* in Norris' novel of that name; Captain Hodgson, keeper of the Fort Point Coast Guard Station and model for Captain Jack in *Blix*, is the man who provided Norris with the inspiration for *Moran of the Lady Letty.*

Before meeting them, Norris had gone in October, 1896, to the Big Dipper Mine near Colfax, California, which his fraternity brother Seymour Waterhouse superintended, to complete *McTeague* and collect material for later short stories. He could, however, find no market for the brutally realistic *McTeague,* and he had to be contented with using some of the characters from the book as the central figures in some short stories for the *Wave* late in 1897 ("Fantaisie Printaniere" and "Judy's Service of Gold Plate"). Norris must have despaired of ever becoming more than a journalist when, from the yarns Captain Hodgson spun, he got the idea for the absurd *Moran of the Lady Letty,* which he began to serialize in the *Wave* of January 8, 1898, before he had even decided how to end it.

Such was the taste of the time that upon reading an installment of this novel of fastidious buccaneering, S. S. McClure, a prominent New York publisher, wrote to offer Norris a position at $12.50 a week for morning work on *McClure's Magazine* that would leave his afternoons free for writing. In February, 1898, Norris arrived in New York City, virtually unknown, to crowd into less than five years a career that would make him one of scarcely more than a half dozen novelists active at the turn of the century whose works would outlive their period. One literary Cinderella had been rescued from the kitchen by a somewhat parsimonious Prince Charming.

II *Dynamo*

One amazing thing is that Norris' sudden success did not go to his head. His fraternity training in self-depreciation and his long-time fears of self-indulgence probably enabled him to take New York in his stride, although we must observe that before he died his writings had brought him more praise than profit.

Within a month after arriving among the four million, Norris met the influential writer who was to be his principal supporter,

William Dean Howells, the Dean of American Letters, whom Norris considered "one of the most delightful men imaginable."[11] Howells offered to read *McTeague* and encouraged Norris to publish it, although it probed into the affairs of a class he had neglected in his own fiction. Meanwhile Norris had brought *Moran of the Lady Letty* to its improbable conclusion and had started work on *Blix*, an optimistic tale probably inspired by his own change of fortune.

Even before *Moran* appeared as a book, however, Norris was off again—with many others—to Cuba to report the Spanish-American War. During his days in the Caribbean, he met the man with whom many critics since Howells have linked his name—Stephen Crane, the other "boy wonder" of American literature. In May, 1899, the two cruised on the *Three Friends,* but they failed to become chummy. Norris wrote rather slightingly of Crane (although not by name) as somewhat "ungenteel" in an unpublished report; neither attempted to resume the acquaintance. Norris' "regular fellow" reluctance to talk about himself and his work probably prevented any effective exchange of ideas between two writers, who could have been very helpful critics to each other. Norris also very likely found the cynical Crane—as rumored—somewhat too "fast" for his fastidious taste, while Crane probably considered Norris something of an ass.

The next month on the fleet flagship Norris met an idol of his college days, Richard Harding Davis, but found him unapproachable. He was more fortunate in striking up an acquaintance with the popular Western artist Frederic Remington. On the whole, the trip was disastrous. Norris' reports were not published, and he was disillusioned by his experiences. The fraternity boy discovered that war is not just a kind of game of lead soldiers or international hazing. Describing, in a letter to Ernest Peixotto, his witnessing of the rape and knifing of a fifteen-year-old girl, Norris protested: "There is precious little glory in war." Yet his ideas about the glorious destiny of the Anglo-Saxons were reinforced. Describing the surrender of Santiago, which he witnessed, he spoke of "the race whose blood instinct is the acquisition of land." The trip also resulted in his contracting malarial fever, which made him too ill to work for several months and may finally have hastened his death.

While he was recuperating in San Francisco, he pursued his decorous romance with Miss Black. Then in September, 1898,

Moran of the Lady Letty at last appeared in print. Reinvigorated by Miss Black's declaration, upon hearing Norris' mother read the novel aloud, that it showed marks of genius, Frank set to work on *A Man's Woman*, which was inspired by Captain Hodgson's experiences in the Arctic. Upon returning to New York to read manuscripts for Frank Doubleday, however, he allowed the novel to bog down into a discussion of the relationship between the sexes.

Things began to move fast. In February, 1899, *McTeague* appeared to the accompaniment of Howells' defense and a chorus of scandalized attacks from entrenched gentility. The next month Norris announced his plans for a vast trilogy about the growth and distribution of wheat. To gather authentic background material for the work, he went back to California and lived for two months on Mr. and Mrs. Gaston Ashe's Santa Anita Ranch near Hollister (not the scene of the novel.) McClure was enthusiastic enough about the project to continue Norris' pay.

He drew upon many sources for this novel—the Mussel Slough affair in 1880; Edwin Markham's sensational poem "The Man with the Hoe" that had just appeared in January, 1899; Isaac Marcosson's knowledge of the kind of deals farmers might put across to get their way with the legislature; tales of Spanish California picked up from ranch workers. During the year that Norris worked on the novel, his financial position improved. He left McClure and became a reader for Frank Doubleday's new corporation at $125 a month, an income that with monthly royalties enabled him at last to marry Jeannette Black on January 12, 1900. The couple took up residence at the Anglesea on famed Washington Square, where they lived until moving in October to a frame cottage in Roselle, New Jersey.

Norris' new position involved him in one of the most sensational controversies in American literary history. Besides works like "Aida of the Coal Mines," which he called in a surviving readers' report "the most damnably bad novel I have ever read,"[12] he was asked to evaluate a manuscript by another ambitious young man with naturalistic leanings. Norris, immensely impressed with Theodore Dreiser's *Sister Carrie*, recommended its publication so strongly that Doubleday offered a contract. A number of versions of what followed exist. Some say that Mrs. Doubleday, some that Doubleday himself was scandalized by the novel. Anyway the firm did try to get out of the contract by attempting to persuade Dreiser that it would not be to his advantage to have the novel published. The author, however, stood fast and so apparently did Norris. The novel was published, but the small edition was effectively suppressed, although Norris managed to send out some review copies.

The loss of Norris' report on *Sister Carrie* is a singular misfortune, for it would be interesting to know what about the book appealed to him. Since it was written in the same vein as *Vandover* and *McTeague*, he may simply have wished to help a fellow experimenter. He must have been disturbed, however, that Carrie's wickedness went unpunished; moreover, Dreiser's stricter determinism must have clashed with Norris' notions about the ultimate triumph of good. A comparison of his books with Dreiser's, though, suggests that what may have been most appealing to Norris in *Sister Carrie* is the picture of Hurstwood's degeneration through self-indulgence, which much resembles McTeague's and Vandover's.

Norris had things on his mind besides justice for Dreiser. He had acquired an English publisher, Grant Richards, and he was obliged to hound him for an accounting. He also completed *The Octopus*, his most ambitious novel, on December 15, 1900. It was published in April, 1901, and enjoyed the largest sale of any to appear during the author's lifetime (33,000 copies of the trade edition.)[13]

Norris had already moved to Chicago to gather material for *The Pit*. He went on to California for a vacation. Back in New York he persuaded George Moulson, a young broker, to continue the education in the intricacies of the futures market that George Gibbs, a fraternity brother, had begun in Chicago. Norris was also busy writing short stories and articles for magazines and a newspaper syndicate. His wife was pregnant.

On February 9, 1902, his daughter Jeannette, Jr., was born, and was soon nicknamed "Billy," in keeping with his penchant for masculine names for his heroines. Soon afterward he finished what was to be his final novel, *The Pit*. He had not enjoyed writing it, and when it was done he denounced New York and decided to leave for good.[14] In July the growing family was back ·in San Francisco, planning a trip around the world on a tramp steamer to collect material for the projected third volume of the wheat trilogy ("The Wolf").

Norris' rejection of the Big City was quite consistent with the distrust of urban civilization expressed in all his books. He also probably felt uncomfortable around the literary crowd he met there. As Franklin Walker observes in Norris' biography, the author "was never a writing man when he was away from his desk."[15] He avoided the "New Bohemians" he satirizes in "Dying Fires," and he spent most of his time with friends from the "old days" of the *Wave*—Bruce Porter, the artist, and Gelett Burgess. He still missed the "Fijis" enough to send a nostalgic dialect poem to the annual dinner at San Francisco's famed Old Poodle Dog restaurant in 1901. Although his job as a reader brought many manuscripts to his desk, the only established writers he became intimate with were the business-like Howells and Hamlin Garland.

The cruise around the world never materialized, for Norris became involved in other matters when he resettled in California. He was already thinking ahead to another trilogy, each volume to describe one of the three days of the Battle of Gettysburg. He exhibited the same courage that he had in his trips to the fighting front and in his aggressive novels, when he came to the defense of an old friend, Dr. William Lawlor, director of the state home for the feeble-minded, who was under attack by the San Francisco press.

Although Lawlor's hearing failed to become the same kind of international sensation as the Dreyfus trial in which Emile Zola was involved, it offered the deprecatingly self-styled "Boy Zola" a chance to show his physical bravery when he pinioned a Colonel Harrington, who drew a revolver during the proceedings. Norris also succeeded in having an article defending Lawlor published as a letter in the *Argonaut*, but the affair ended with the doctor's honorable dismissal.

Norris became the center of a smaller tempest when both he and Jack London, whom he never met, published short stories about a man killed by a dog retrieving a stick of dynamite. (Norris' version, "The Passing of Cock-Eye Blacklock," is preserved in *A Deal in Wheat and Other Stories.*) Charges of plagiarism were hurled about, but there is little reason to question either man's assertion that they worked independently from a newspaper account of an actual event.

Norris was also house-hunting. After visiting Robert Louis Stevenson's widow in the Santa Cruz Mountains, he began negotiating to buy a property near hers to be called *Quien Sabe?* (Who knows?) after the college-bred Annixter's ranch in *The Octopus.* But Norris was never to enjoy the country living he had so long extolled in his fiction. In October, 1902, while his wife was recuperating from an appendicitis operation, he was stricken with an abdominal pain. He paid no attention to it; but on the twenty-fifth of the month he was dead of a perforated appendix and peritonitis.

His two attacks of tropical fever and his general neglect of himself had weakened Norris' system. The two futile quests for foreign adventure had very likely in the long run destroyed the man who as a young student had dreamed of chivalric adventure. The writer who his biographer justifiably stated was made great by his "boyish qualities" was dead—leaving an estate estimated at only one thousand dollars.[16] To judge from the posthumously published *Pit,* he died on what might have proved to be the verge of intellectual and artistic maturity.

III *A Long Shadow*

No influential writer's story ends with his death. Only a quarter of *The Pit* had been serialized in the *Saturday Evening Post* when the author died. When published the next year, the novel became his outstanding success, selling nearly a hundred thousand copies in the original trade edition. It reached an even wider audience in 1904 when Channing Pollock fashioned it into a Broadway play that ran for seventy-seven performances. In 1917, William A. Brady, who had produced the play, made it into a motion picture starring Wilton Lackaye, who had played Jadwin on the stage, and new readers enjoyed a special "tie-in" edition of the novel containing stills suggesting how the film caught the gaudy style of Norris' era. The book also reputedly supplied the name for a popular card game.

No record exists of other plays having been produced from Norris' novels, but several were filmed, even though Hollywood has not fully exploited the author's works. In 1922 *Moran of the Lady Letty* was adapted to the talents of the rising matinee idol, Rudolph Valentino, and in 1924, Norris provided the basis for one of the most ambitious motion pictures of the silent era. His *McTeague,* which had already been filmed once in 1915 under the title *Life's Whirlpool,* was chosen as a vehicle by the perfectionist director Erich von Stroheim, who attempted absolute fidelity to Norris' text. The ten-hour long motion picture had to be slashed without its director's consent for commercial release, but even in its mutilated form, *Greed* has frequently been hailed as one of the great classics of cinematic realism.[17]

Meanwhile Norris' devoted brother Charles strove to keep Frank's memory alive and to add to his reputation. Finally in 1914, *Vandover and the Brute*—its manuscript preserved from the San Francisco fire—was published with additions and an introduction by Charles. In 1928, the tenth volume of the Collected Works included some previously unpublished work and many short stories and articles that had hitherto been available only in rare periodicals. Still more of Norris' fugitive pieces were gathered in 1931 in *Frank Norris of the Wave*, for which both Charles Norris and book-collector Oscar Lewis provided informative introductions. Most of Norris' critical essays had been collected in 1903 under the title *Responsibilities of the Novelist*.

Norris' brother did not devote himself exclusively to preserving his brother's work; probably inspired by Frank's example, Charles—who had already followed his elder brother into Phi Gamma Delta and an editorial career—tried his own hand at fiction and produced nearly a dozen novels; their titles—usually a single word like *Brass, Bread, Seed*—indicate their distinctly didactic purpose. Charles was never to enjoy anything like his flamboyant brother's reputation. The weakness of his work is that pointed out in Frank's essay, "The Novel with a Purpose," for Charles cared more for the points he was trying to make than for his story: "Result—sermons . . . , special pleading, a farrago of dry, dull incidents, overburdened and collapsing under the weight of a theme that should have intruded only indirectly."

The same thing can surely not be said of the vast amount of fiction produced by the third of the writing Norrises—Charles's wife Kathleen, one of America's best known popular writers and for decades the darling of sentimental readers of *Collier's* and the *Woman's Home Companion*. Although scorned by academic critics, the author of *Mother* has probably made the name Norris familiar to and beloved by more readers than the two reform-minded brothers combined.

Frank Norris' wife remarried and lived for many years after him, avoiding the limelight. She remained devoted, however, to the impetuous young fraternity man who emblazoned his name on his country's literary history. In 1942 she attended the dedication of a ship named for this man who had written so excitedly of the sea, and even in the 1950's, when ill in a nursing home, she assisted the University of California's Bancroft Library in its effort to bring together Norris' scattered papers and books for the use of the college English professors he scorned.

CHAPTER *2*

March We Must

NEAR THE END of *The Octopus* occurs one of the most troublesome passages in Norris' work: "Men—motes in the sunshine—perished, were shot down in the very noon of life, hearts were broken, little children started in life lamentably handicapped. . . . In that little, isolated group of human insects, misery, death, and anguish spun like a wheel of fire" (*Collected Works*, 11, 360).°

This coolly impersonal description of men as "motes in the sunshine" is difficult to reconcile with Norris' emphatic statement elsewhere that "*In the last analysis the people are always right*" (VII, 222). It is also difficult to square the announcement that the novelist's story "will be to him as impersonal a thing as the key is to the composer of a sonata," which Norris concedes is "a selfish view of the question" (VII, 23-24), with his other assertion that "the better the personal morality of the writer, the better his writings" (VII, 218). For it is difficult to see why, if the novelist is not personally concerned about his subject, his private morality should have anything to do with his treatment of it.

Seeming contradictions like these have led to Norris' thinking being attacked as inconsistent. We might reply with Emerson's dictum, "a foolish consistency is the hobgoblin of little minds," but it is more profitable to seek principles that unify Norris' diversified utterances.

I deliberately quote Emerson because Norris' thought, closely

° Unless otherwise identified, references to Norris' works are to the ten-volume Collected Edition, Garden City, New York, 1928. Subsequent references to this edition will be incorporated into the text with only volume and page numbers given.

examined, remarkably—although apparently coincidentally—resembles some transcendentalist credos. Far from being an exotic whose affinities are principally with French naturalists, Norris is a Far West answer to the call from Concord—a writer who hoped to break New World dependence upon the Old. When we reconstruct from his critical writings his philosophy of man and nature, we learn how congenial the dynamic spokesmen of two widely separated American generations might have found each other. Before examining Norris' fiction, we need to be acquainted with the theories behind it.

The posthumous collection *Responsibilities of a Novelist* (1903) contains two kinds of material—what can best be described as pedagogical and polemical essays. Most of the former, like "New York as a Literary Center" and "The Mechanics of Fiction," which were written for a newspaper syndicate, are interesting period pieces that suggest how successful Norris might have been as an instructor in creative writing, but they give us no very informative glimpse into the artist's mind at work. The first seven essays in the book and a scattering of others (especially "A Problem in Fiction" and "Simplicity in Art"), which originally appeared in magazines like *The Critic* and *World's Work*, are apparently rather hurried but quite vehement statements of the novelist's artistic creed. They are not entirely consistent with each other, and they are somewhat chaotically constructed; but these seeming defects may actually be advantages from the critic's viewpoint since they allow him to look behind some of the surface exhortations at the assumptions that prompted them. Thoughtful revision can be mixed blessing; for, while polishing may eliminate inconsistencies, it may also obscure motives.

Norris' principal contention is that the novelist should tell the *truth*; but he is not very explicit about how the truth is to be recognized. "Responsibilities of a Novelist," the essay that gives the collection its title, insists that "the people have a right to the Truth," and that it is essential that the novelist tell it. Yet although Norris denounces those who exploit and deceive the public with "false views of life, false characters, false sentiment, false morality, false history, false philosophy, false emotions, false heroism, false notions of self-sacrifice, false views of religion, of duty, of conduct, of manners" (VII, 9), he is never specific about how the truth may be distinguished from these widespread falsehoods. In "The True Reward of the Novelist," he goes on to say only that the novelist should write to tell the truth, not to make money but again he says nothing about the nature of the truth.

"The Novel with a Purpose" is less vague. Answering those who protest that since there is so much suffering in the world, they do not want it in novels, Norris says: "If there is much pain in life, all the more reason that it should appear in a class of literature which, in its highest form, is a sincere transcription of life" (VII, 25). In this essay he also makes the somewhat puzzling statement that if "the page-to-page progress" of *Uncle Tom's Cabin* had not been more absorbing to Harriet Beecher Stowe "than all the Negroes that were ever whipped or sold," she would not have succeeded in the "great purpose" of the novel. The truth Norris is concerned about is thus indicated not to be the "facts" about a given situation, but fidelity to "human nature."

That this idea is what he does have in mind he states as explicitly as he ever does in "A Problem in Fiction," which contains the assertion that "truth" and "accuracy" are not the same thing. Denying that if one describes just what he sees he is truthful, Norris writes seemingly paradoxically, "Life itself is not always true; strange as it may seem, you may be able to say that life is not always true to life—from the point of view of the artist." He attempts to clear up what he means by explaining:

> In the fine arts we do not care one little bit about what life actually is, but what it looks like to an interesting, impressionable man, and if he tells his story or paints his picture so that the majority of intelligent people will say, "Yes, that must have been just about what would have happened under those circumstances," he is true. . . . He need not be accurate if he does not choose to be. If he sees fit to be inaccurate in order to make his point—so only his point be the conveying of a truthful impression—that is his affair (VII, 172-73).

From the literalist's standpoint, of course, this statement is sheer nonsense, and the scientifically minded critic would be obliged to dismiss it as wishful thinking. It is entirely intelligible, however, in the light of the kind of Platonic thinking that we find among the American transcendentalists, who view general principles as more important than particular cases. A good example is Thoreau's reaction to newspaper stories about disasters: "If you are acquainted with the principle, what do you care for a myriad instances and applications?" Norris' statement that "Accuracy is the attainment of small minds" (VII, 174) distinctly recalls Emerson on consistency. It also foreshadows the thinking of those twentieth-century artists who maintain that art is "presentational" rather than "representational," and may indicate a generally unnoted link between their ideas and transcendentalism.

Nor was this idea just a passing fancy of Norris'. He had entertained it at least as early as November, 1896, when he had the author of a series of "Dramas of the Curbstone" (a title Norris himself used) remark when told that something he might use in a story had really happened: "That don't help matters any if it don't read like real life. . . . It's not the things that have really happened that make good fiction, but the things that read as though they had."[1]

This interest in principles rather than particulars explains how the passages quoted at the beginning of this chapter may be reconciled. Norris can speak with apparent callousness of men as "motes in the sunshine" and still speak passionately of the correctness of the common people, if he is speaking of the triumph of virtue in the long, not the short run. He would be inspired by the same sentiment that has so long disturbed impatient reformers with Walt Whitman's "Nay, Tell Me Not To-day the Publish'd Shame"—that not all temporary evils can be eliminated. How can Norris, on the one hand, say that if Hardy were to write a novel about injustices to coal miners and "remain an artist," he would "as a novelist, care very little about the iniquitous labor system of the Welsh coal mines" (VII, 23) and yet, on the other hand, reject the idea that "the personal morality of the artist . . . has nothing to do with his work" (VII, 218)? Norris can, if he thinks that the artist must be motivated by virtuous principles, but must also concentrate upon his own work and not fritter away his energies trying to eliminate particular evils in the world. His ideas parallel the contrast Thoreau makes in *Walden* between *goodness* as "the only investment that never fails" and *doing-good* as "one of the professions which are full."

If Norris was—perhaps not even consciously—committed to such ideas, we would expect to find in his writings statements that he believed in some kind of transcendent order in nature, like the Emersonian "oversoul," to which man in his ideal state is attuned. Looking back beyond the transcendentalist into the eighteenth century, we would even expect to find Norris sharing with Pope the idea of an "unerring" order of nature, "one clear, unchang'd, and universal light . . . at once the source, and end, and test of art" (*Essay on Criticism*, ll. 71-74).[2] Scattered through his writings, we find exactly this, although it would not be safe to look to Emerson, Pope, or those who influenced them as specific sources for these ideas.

There is, of course, the famous statement at the end of *The Octopus* that "through all shams, all wickednesses . . . all things surely, inevitably, resistlessly work together for good" (II, 361); but, unsupported, this could be dismissed as an excited artist's metaphoric rationalization of his refusal to accept as final the distressing truth about a dismal situation. In his discussion, "The Great American Novelist," however, Norris makes a much more literal statement that confirms his belief in some kind of beneficent universal order:

> If an American novelist should go so deep into the lives of the people of any one community that he would find the thing that is common to another class of people a thousand miles away, he would have gone *too* deep to be exclusively American. He would not only be American, but English as well. He would have sounded the world note. He would be a writer not national but international, and his countrymen would be all humanity, not the citizens of any one nation. He himself would be a heritage of the whole world, A second Tolstoi . . . (VII, 67).

Norris is expressing in this statement sentiments similar to those with which Pope climaxes his "Essay on Man," describing how self-love leads the individual from friend, parent, neighbor, country to "all human race" until ultimately "th' o'erflowings of the mind take ev'ry creature in of ev'ry kind" (Epistle IV, 361-70).

When we find Norris thus theorizing about universal brotherhood, we are obliged to ask, however, how he could have also made those statements about Anglo-Saxon superiority that some critics have found among the most distasteful things he said. In *The Octopus*, for example, he writes, "The Anglo-Saxon spectators round about drew back in disgust, but the hot degenerated blood of Portuguese, Mexican, and mixed Spaniard boiled up in excitement at this wholesale slaughter [of jack-rabbits the Anglo-Saxons have ordered rounded up]" (II, 214). And ". . . and honest Anglo-Saxon mirth and innocence commended [the group]. . . . These people were good people. . . . They were good stock" (II, 216). In "The Frontier Gone at Last," he writes that "a hundred thousand of the more hardy rushed to the skirmish line and went at the wilderness as only the Anglo-Saxon can" and "the Anglo-Saxon in his course of empire had circled the globe and brought the new civilization to the old civilization" (VII, 54-55).

It is hard to reconcile such bellowings of racial pride with the question at the end of the same essay: "Will it not go on, this epic of civilization, this destiny of the races, until at last and at the ultimate end of all we who now arrogantly boast ourselves as Americans . . . may realize that the true patriotism is the brotherhood of man and know that the whole world is our nation and simple humanity our countrymen?" (VII, 61). Nor was the last sentiment simply a passing thought. Norris had expressed it in an account in 1897 of a colonization scheme that proposed to make a White Man's Eden of the "cannibal" island of Bougainville in the South Pacific (X, 86-88).

The statements strike modern readers as antagonistic because of our bitter experiences with the Nazis and other racists; they have led us to suspect that all who speak of racial superiority are hate-mongers obsessed with and determined to preserve the notion that men are inherently and immutably divided into "superior" and "inferior" groups. Norris' thinking has nothing in common, however, with that of intransigent South African advocates of "apartheid" or with the Ku Klux Klan view of the permanent necessity of preserving racial purity. Norris himself had little enthusiasm for the Boers, whom he described as "sluggish, unambitious, unenergetic, unspeakably stupid" (x, 231); and in "The National Spirit as It Relates to the Great American Novel," he denounced American sectionalism.[3]

One of his criticisms of "degenerate" Spanish blood is actually an endorsement of racial mixing. In "A Case for Lombroso," he says that Crescencia Hromada's sensitivity was "morbid and unnatural," because "she had come of a family of unmixed blood, whose stock has never been replenished or strengthened by an alien cross. Her race was almost exhausted, its vitality low, and its temperament refined to the evaporation point" (X, 36).

Norris' notions of Anglo-Saxon superiority are thus based not on *a priori* assumptions but on observation. Possibly his observations were biased and unscientific, but they were altruistic; his dream was of bringing all peoples up to the level of the superior groups, not of exploiting "inferior" ones. While perhaps smugly naïve, these are the *dynamic* views of a man who believed that the world could and should be improved for everybody—not the *static* views of the "White Supremacist," who seeks to preserve a status quo favorable to a selected few.

The dynamism of Norris' views is, in fact, indicated by the grounds upon which he rests his concept of Anglo-Saxon superiority. He lauds the "race" for its constant broaching of new frontiers: "The race impulse was irresistible. March we must, conquer we must, and checked in the westward course of empire, we turned eastward and expended the resistless energy that by blood was ours in conquering the old world behind us" (VII, 55). The key phrase is "the resistless energy that by blood was ours." Norris elaborates upon this idea:

> To-day we are the same race, with the same impulse . . . and because there is no longer a Frontier to absorb our overplus of energy, because there is no longer a wilderness to conquer, and because we still must march, still must conquer, we remember the old days when our ancestors . . . turned their faces eastward. . . . No sooner have we found that our path to the westward has ended then, reacting eastward, we are at the Old World again . . . devoting our overplus of energy to its subjugation (VII, 56).

Although Norris does not specifically say so, it is obvious that what is wrong with the "degenerate" races is that they fail to be dynamic (he was probably thinking especially of Spain's failure to hold on to and develop its American colonial empire).

The important thing is that this impulse, which Norris also calls a "blood instinct," is involuntary and unconscious. "Races must follow their destiny blindly," he continues. Charles Walcutt speaks of Norris' reliance upon "mystical natural dynamism" in *The Pit*, but the term applies not so much to the views underlying that novel as to Norris' whole basic philosophy. For to

Norris the superior man or race is the one instinctively in step with the ceaseless, forward movement of the universe.

When we arrive at last at the term *destiny*, however, we reach the point where Norris' thought does become uncertain and vacillating, since he was never able to satisfy himself about the prime mover of this destiny. He was not a consistent scientific determinist, like some Continental naturalists, for in essays like "A Plea for Romantic Fiction" and "Simplicity in Art," he can speak of God with the warmth of a Holiness preacher. Yet at the same time he distinctly rejects any notions of predetermination in the narrow sense of an individual "calling":

> Given the ordinarily intelligent ten-year-old and, all things being equal, you can make anything you like out of him—a minister of the gospel or a green-goods man, an electrical engineer or a romantic poet. . . . If a failure is the result, blame the method of training, not the quantity or quality of the ten-year-old's intellect. Don't say, if he is a failure as a fine novelist, that he lacks genius for writing and would have been a fine business man. Make no mistake, if he did not have enough "genius" for novel-writing, he would certainly have not had enough for business (VII, 98).

Such statements were probably designed partly to rationalize Norris' rejection of a business career, but they could proceed only from a notion that there is a motive power in the universe that endows men with an "instinct" or "genius" not for some particular task, but simply for dynamic, creative action. It is then up to men to direct this "genius" into useful channels, possibly according to the needs of the times.

The very vagueness of this concept of "genius" made it possible for Norris to settle for himself the old controversy over the existence of free will in a purposeful universe. If man's destiny is simply to use the "genius" he is endowed with to work toward "good," without this "genius" being preassigned any specific function, the extent of his possible accomplishment is predetermined. But he is left free to choose to use his ability as he will or even not to use it at all.

These remarks do not just record a transient idea; in "The True Reward of the Novelist," Norris had observed:

You [the novelist] must be something more . . . than just a
writer. There must be that nameless sixth sense or sensibility
in you that great musicians have in common with great inven-
tors and great scientists; the thing that does not enter into the
work, but that is back of it; the thing that would make of you a
good *man* as well as a good novelist; the thing that differentiates
the mere business man from the financier (for it is possessed of
the financier and poet alike—so only they be big enough)
(VII, 17).

Norris refers also in *The Octopus* to a kind of "sixth sense" that
gives man the ability to penetrate directly to the heart of things
with the unclouded vision that Emerson would have called the
ability to receive revelation directly from the "oversoul," but
the particular points of interest in the passage from the essay
are the equation of the "good novelist" with the "good man"
and the idea that "big" men in different fields have more in
common than "big" and "little" men in the same field.

Norris could become quite heated about the interrelation of
moral and professional goodness. One of the clearest disclosures
of his fundamental assumptions is found in the long paragraph
in "Salt and Sincerity" about Madame Humbert, a notorious
French confidence woman:

There is a certain journal of the Middle West of the United
States which has proclaimed, with a great flourish of trumpets,
that Mme. Humbert of Paris would have made a great "fictionist"
if she had not elected to become a great swindler . . . it is the
contention that the personal morality of the artist (including
"fictionists") has nothing to do with his work, and that a great
rascal may be a good painter, good musician, good novelist.
With painters, musicians, and the like this may or may not be
true. With the novelist one contends, believes, and avers that
it is absolutely and unequivocally false, and that the mind
capable of theft, of immorality, of cruelty, of foulness, of false-
ness of any kind, is incapable, under any circumstances, or by
any degree of stimulation, of producing one single important,
artistic, or useful piece of fiction. The better the personal morality
of the writer, the better his writings . . . it is not the ingenious
criminal, who is the novelist *manqué*, but the philanthropist,
the great educator, the great pulpit orator, the great statesman.
It is from such stuff that the important novels are made, not
from the deranged lumber and disordered claptrap of the brain
of a defective (VII, 217-19).

Only by studying this statement carefully do we perceive the specific link between Norris' theories of man and of fiction. Unmistakably, he felt that the great novelist is a man of genius who might have successfully followed any profession that he chose. The fact that the genius is innate and the profession chosen accounts for Norris' anti-intellectual theories of education. All that schooling can provide, he felt, is technique.

Advocates of liberal arts training can find scant consolation in Norris' work, for he stands at the extreme end of the spectrum from men like Robert Hutchins. Norris advocates purely technical training. *The Octopus* is devoted, among other things, to proving that none of the three college men who play principal roles in it—Annixter, Vanamee, Presley—learned anything about life until they left school. Harvard starts Vandover on the road to ruin; the hero of *Moran of the Lady Letty* learns more from the heroine who received all her training at sea than he did from Yale; Blix asks "isn't studying medicine . . . better than piano-playing, or French courses, or literary classes and Browning circles?" Among the "Salt and Sincerity" papers is a long attack on conventional scholarship including this prophecy:

> One chooses to believe that the college of the end of the present century will be an institution where only specialized work will be indulged in. There will be courses in engineering, in electricity, in agriculture, in law . . . etc., and the so-called general "literary" or "classical" courses will be relegated to the limbo of Things No Longer Useful. . . . The man who studies law at college finishes his work a lawyer, he who studies engineering ends an engineer. . . . But the student in the "literary" courses does not——no, not once in a thousand instances, graduate a literary man. He spends the four years of his life over a little Greek, a little Latin, a little mathematics, a little literature, a little history, a little "theme" writing, and comes out—just what it would be difficult to say (VII, 203).

In "Novelists to Order," on the other hand, Norris defends instruction in creative writing (VII, 97-101), and it is noteworthy that when, after his academically unsatisfactory years in Berkeley, he went to Harvard, he took only a course which gave him a chance to write creatively. His distrust of "liberal" education is not difficult to reconcile with his theory of "natural goodness." His view was that men did not need to be trained to be "good" men, but only to function effectively at a specialized task.

What instruction men need in goodness, they could receive
from the "good" geniuses, particularly the novelists. Norris'
lofty concept of the role of his own chosen vehicle is set forth
in "Responsibilities of the Novelist." In the first place, he held
that the novel was to be to the twentieth century what archi-
tecture had been to the Middle Ages and painting and drama to
the Renaissance: "To-day is the day of the novel . . . the critics
of the twenty-second century, reviewing our times, striving to
reconstruct our civilization, will look not to the painters, not
to the architects nor dramatists, but to the novelists to find
our idiosyncrasy" (VII, 4). The novel, furthermore, was the
most influential of the three "great moulders of public opinion
and public morals to-day," because of the other two—the Pulpit
"speaks but once a week" and the Press "is read with lightning
haste" (VII, 8). Norris thus saw the novelist as the most influential single force in keeping men moving resistlessly toward
the good.

The "purpose" he assigns the novel thus becomes manifest;
the novelist must not allow himself to become involved in
particular situations because he must keep his eyes focused
constantly on the universal principles of goodness that transcend
individual and partisan considerations. He must be moved, as
Richard Chase says Norris himself was, "most deeply . . . not
by people and their daily tragedies and adventures, but by
abstractions, by Forces, Environments, Accidents, and Influences,"[4] by what Norris himself would prefer to call "the Great
March." The novelist must not be a special pleader; he must
not allow his private preferences to intrude into his art. As
adamant as Henry James in "The Art of Fiction" on this point,
Norris insisted that "the preaching, the moralizing, is the result
not of direct appeal by the writer, but is made—should be
made—to the reader by the very incidents of the story" (VII, 23).

He states quite explicitly in "Simplicity in Art" the thoroughly
romantic viewpoint that the author must not tell the reader
what to think about the action; he must let events speak for
themselves: "Comment is superfluous. If the author makes the
scene appear terrible to the reader he need not say in himself
or in the mouth of some protagonist, 'It is terrible!' . . . If beautiful, we do not want him to tell us so. We want him to make
it beautiful, and our own appreciation will supply the adjectives"
(VII, 188).

Norris was calling, in short, for the kind of fusion of incident and meaning that John Steinbeck achieved in works like *Of Mice and Men* and *The Red Pony*, but which Norris himself failed to achieve with any consistency in his own work. Norris concerned himself, like Henry James, with telling his story, feeling that if he made it "interesting," the "moral" would take care of itself. Reviewing a novel by Elizabeth Tompkins, he wrote in the *Wave* in July, 1896: "A romance may, of course, have excitement and brilliancy and any number of attractive things, but there is one quality it absolutely must have—that which prevents you from putting it down when you have once begun it."

This theorizing of Norris about the presentation of a novel accords remarkably well with currently fashionable critical dicta derived from Henry James. The most striking thing about Norris is that he coupled remarkably sophisticated theories about the writing of fiction with almost staggeringly naïve notions about "instincts," "sixth senses," "superior races," and "natural good-ness," and this characteristic illustrates that it was literary tech-niques and not philosophy that he borrowed from the naturalists. By clinging to old ideas, he himself quite unwittingly illustrated the source of much distress in the contemporary world—the shortcomings of the very kind of man he advocated who had excellent technical training and no liberal education.

Franklin Walker says that Norris' greatness lies in his "boyish" qualities. Walker is right, but he fails to observe that boyishness is not enough where there is a man's job to be done. The source of Norris' greatness is also his outstanding weakness; for through most of his career he remained an overgrown boy, and like most boys he displayed more enthusiasm for his ideas than understanding of what they meant.

Whether, for example, he really attempted to understand what he meant by "good" is doubtful. He had little use for re-flective thinking. Praising "story-tellers" as opposed to "novelists," Norris wrote that the men and women of the storyteller's world "are not apt to be—to him—so important in themselves as in relation to the whirl of things in which he chooses to involve them. . . . His work is haphazard. . . . He does not *know*; he *feels*" (VII, 32). Norris expresses this preference for thinking over feeling frequently in his novels; in part it develops out of his theory that "every healthy-minded child . . . is a story-teller"

and that "sometimes the little story-teller does not die, but lives
on and grows with the man, increasing in favour with God, till
at last he dominates the man himself" (VII, 31).

This idolization of perpetual childhood carries us back beyond
transcendentalism to the Wordsworth of the "Intimations of Im-
mortality" Ode. The idea that the child has a "purer" vision than
the adult is unmistakable in the peroration of Norris' essay on
"story-tellers":

> . . . unless the child vision and the child pleasure be present to
> guide and to stimulate, the entrances of the kingdom must stay
> forever shut to those who would enter, storm they the gates
> never so mightily. . . . Without the auxiliary of the little play-
> mate of the old days the great doors . . . will stay forever shut.
> Look once, however, with the child's eye, or for once touch the
> mighty valves with the child's hand, and heaven itself lies open
> with all its manifold wonders (VII, 34).

Norris thus exalts childhood more than once. In "The Need
for a Literary Conscience," he writes that while in science and
finance leaders may have to be strong, sure men, in literature
greatness ". . . will come to you, if it comes at all, because you
shall have kept yourself young and humble and pure in heart, and
so unspoiled and unwearied and unjaded that you shall find a
joy in the mere rising of the sun . . . shall see God in a little
child and a whole religion in a brooding bird" (VII, 41). Hand-
in-hand with this praise of childhood goes a suspicion of civilization. Writing about the "Master Note," to which "the silver
cord of our creative faculty" responds, Norris warns in one of
his most bathetic passages that this note "will not be heard
within 'commuting distance of the city,'" because "the whir of
civilization smothers it." Its pursuit rather, he advises, leads to
"untracked, uncharted corners of the earth" (VII, 208-9).

Behind such theories, by no means unique with Norris, lies a
hatred of growing up. The figure that at last emerges from the
fuzzy whirl of Norris' exuberant philosophizing as a kind of ideal
for the human race is Peter Pan, and the instinctive march
Norris hails is really the flight from mature responsibility and
even from reality. Escapist fiction is, of course, no novelty;
hacks produce it by the bale to feed the delusions of millions of
would-be Peter Pans. Most such romancers simply exploit for-
mulas to make money. A genuinely escapist writer who really

believes in his own fantasies is, however, a quite unusual phenomenon, for very few drug addicts have the energy or know-how to raise their own crop. An escapist fascinated by the techniques of scientific naturalism is a curious specimen indeed, since he sweeps into the heart of the opposing camp to borrow its tools without listening to its theories about their use. His work is not likely to lend itself to simple interpretation.

Actually Norris was most fortunate in that he was too moralistically inclined to carry out his own theories about the indifference of the artist to his subject. Had he achieved the objectivity he talked about with no more mature philosophy than he possessed, he would have written—as he did in some of his contributions to the *Wave*—the kind of violent, meaningless sensationalism with which paperbound bookstalls are loaded today.

In my preface, I say that Norris owes more to naturalism than it does to him. Had he not been an escapist at all, he might have produced a "tough-minded" fiction that would have shocked America's genteel literary society so much as to produce reactions that would make those elicited by *McTeague* and *Sister Carrie* pale indeed. Had Norris, on the other hand, been only an escapist, he probably would never have abandoned the Middle Ages, but would have been content like many of his contemporaries with the illusionary world of costume romance—with the result that his novels would now be as dead as theirs.

Since he was what he was, his work has a distinctive value as the reflection of a mind that resented and feared a maturity that was being thrust upon it. Until he had recognized the need for coming to terms with this inevitable maturity (and he was apparently beginning to recognize it when he wrote *The Pit*), he could not have intentionally produced work that would much enlighten others. Yet as long as he was in the throes of the struggle he could unintentionally generate great light on problems of fundamental importance to ages besides his own. The most accurate way to sum up Frank Norris is to say that he was a moralist in spite of himself.

Young Man's Fancy

I *Long Ago and Far Away*

MOST CRITICS have justifiably skipped over the published souvenirs of Norris' student days, but apprentice work cannot be entirely ignored if we are to have an over-all view of a writer's development. Norris' earliest work is especially interesting since, as a result of his adolescent infatuation with the Middle Ages, it is drastically different in style and content from the fiction upon which his reputation rests. Yet when we strip away the medieval armor, as heroic Sir Cavarlaye does at one critical point in *Yvernelle*, we find that in theme and tone these efforts foreshadow what will follow.

The most ambitious of Norris' early works is *Yvernelle*, three cantos of iambic tetrameter couplets that were published with a subsidy from the author's mother as an elaborately illustrated Christmas gift book in 1891. Since the poetry is amateurish, the most striking feature of *Yvernelle* is its unabashed morality. Best described as "The Old Homestead" on oven-aged parchment, the poem sings of a wicked Spanish temptress, Guhaldrada, who places a curse on the next lips that press those of one of her bumpkin victims from the French countryside. The hero's nuptials are temporarily delayed when his refusal to buss his betrothed is misconstrued and her guardian orders him away. Virtue triumphs, however, for the curse falls back threefold upon Guhaldrada, when—as a result of her scheming— she loses her beauty, her brother, and her band of loyal retainers. Justice done at the end of Canto Two, there is nothing left to occupy the third part of the poem but the frantic ride to prevent the heroine from taking disastrous vows—in this tale as a nun. The material would make a wonderful movie, but producers can be excused for not having perceived the story beneath the panoply of cumbersome verse. The book was generally ignored, but, never a man to waste a plot, Norris used this one again nine years later in a prose short story, "The Riding of Felipe."

The most interesting feature of *Yvernelle* is a seemingly irrelevant foreword in which Norris compares villainous feudal barons to the crooked entrepreneurs of his own day:

> The feudal baron yet remains to-day,
> But, changed into the modern moneyed lord,
> Still o'er the people holds more cruel sway,
> But 'tis with hoarded gold and not with sword.
> Still do his vassals feel his iron heel.
> His power awes—his government alarms;
> Still rings the world with sound of clashing steel;
> 'Tis of machinery and not of arms (VI, 251).

Although this passage foreshadows one of Jack London's catchiest titles, it provides no clue to an allegorical interpretation that adds any weight to the poem—unless Guhaldrada is Steve Canyon's Cooper Calhoon in disguise. The comment does show, however, that even during his college days, despite his conservative upbringing and associates, Norris was even more suspicious of industrial titans than later when he speaks favorably of San Francisco's industrialists in *A Man's Woman* and *The Octopus*.

An example of his acceptance while a student of an idea that persists to become a keynote in his work, is the statement "The merits of an age are all its own/ Its evils are those common to mankind," in which Norris equates *dynamism* with *goodness*, on the one hand, and a *static* condition with *evil*, on the other. The identification even at the beginning of his literary career of change with virtue shows a fundamental progressiveness that would have made Norris sympathetic to novel, fictional techniques like Zola's naturalism. It shows also his basic romanticism, since the lines can serve as a statement of the difference between the archetypal classic and romantic viewpoints.

Fortunately, Norris soon lost interest in his rendezvous with the past. His prose tales of the Middle Ages are not memorable. "The Jongleur of Taillebois" is an artfully constructed horror-revenge story of the kind that used to appear in *Weird Tales* and the other macabre pulp magazines. But "Lauth," which is evidently intended to make the distinctly un-naturalistic point that while man is not much different from beasts his small distinction is that he possesses a soul, is one of the most ineptly told tales ever preserved between boards.

The most interesting of Norris' undergraduate concoctions is "Son of a Sheik," which is more nearly essay than short story. Bab Azzoun, a noble Arab turned Parisian boulevardier, utters nearly the same sentiments that Norris himself did later, in "The Frontier Gone at Last":

> "Patriotism has passed through five distinct stages; first it was only love of family . . . then, as the family grows and expands into the tribe, it becomes the object of affection. . . . In the third stage . . . patriotism is devotion to the city. . . . In the next period, patriotism means affection for the state . . . while we of today form the latest, but not the last, link of the lengthening chain by honouring, loving and serving the *country*. . . . Yet I do not believe this to be the last, the highest, the noblest form of patriotism. . . . This development shall go on . . . until . . . we attain to that height from which we can look down upon the world as our country, humanity as our countrymen . . ." (IV, 70-71).

His fellow travelers are not impressed, and at the end of the story Bab Azzoun himself identifies with some Kabyle tribesmen attacking the French. "In an instant," the narrator explains, "all the long years of culture and education were stripped away as a garment." Bab Azzoun leaps from the boat and is never seen again by his civilized colleagues. Even this early Norris is concerned about the slender hold civilization has upon man. How close to the surface the savage in us lies is to become the subject of his first important writings.

Even before he migrated to Harvard in 1895 to study creative writing, Norris had returned home from the Middle Ages. His first preserved ventures into contemporary realism are stories that he sold to the *Overland Monthly*, once Bret Harte's magazine. Most of these are superficial pieces in the style that O. Henry made famous; the only impressive thing about them is the economy of the author's style. They can be exemplified by "Travis Hallett's Half-Back," which tells how a football player proves the value of his sport by using a trick he learned on the playing field to rescue his girl friend from a burning theatre.

The worst that can be said for Norris' stories of this period is that they are cloyingly sentimental. We could hardly have predicted the controversial course of the author's career from such tales as "Toppan" and "A Caged Lion," which concern a daring explorer whom a society girl domesticates, for they seem models for the kind of endearing fiction about the soothing influence of a good woman that made Norris' sister-in-law Kathleen the darling of the *Woman's Home Companion* for several decades. He needed a fresh inspiration if he were to become more than an agile hack.

II *His Own Backyard*

The combined influence of Emile Zola and Lewis Gates was enough to lift Norris almost completely out of the ranks of the literary tricksters after his arrival at Harvard and to enable him to devise his first unmistakably tractarian work. Since he worked on both *Vandover and the Brute* and *McTeague* in Cambridge, precedence between the novels has never been straightened out. Charles Norris thought that *McTeague* was begun and largely completed before the other novel was even started, but he also admitted that *McTeague* is the product of a more mature mind. Since it was revised and seen through the press by the author, while *Vandover* (which did not appear until 1914) was never published under his supervision, we are justified in treating the "lost" novel as the last of Norris' apprentice works and *McTeague* (published in 1899) as his first effort as a professional craftsman.

Even in the unsatisfactory form in which it has reached us, *Vandover and the Brute* is obviously a tract against self-indulgence. Norris must have been especially uneasy about this "evil" when he went to Harvard, for he may have felt roistering was responsible for his failures as a painter and as a student. Self-indulgence would also be especially heinous to one who held the puritanical view expressed in *Yvernelle* that evil is inherited and merit acquired, since it would represent a failure to respond to Nature's dynamic promptings. The story cannot, however, be satisfactorily interpreted autobiographically. Norris exploited himself, his family, and his friends for realistic material, but he altered events so much that any conclusions drawn about his attitude towards specific persons would be far-fetched. He probably intended the novel as a warning to himself as well as others, and he depended more upon his fertile imagination than upon his limited experience in devising the succession of powerful scenes in the story.

The tale is episodic, but gripping. Vandover is the motherless son of a wealthy owner of San Francisco slum properties. He thinks he wants to be an artist, but he cannot discipline himself to work. In an idle moment he seduces an equally frivolous young woman, whose shame drives her to suicide. The revelation of Vandover's responsibility for her death kills his father. Left to his own devices, Vandover proves incapable of either pursuing his career or managing his patrimony. Ostensible friends cheat him of part of his fortune; he squanders the rest, particularly in gambling. Finally he becomes a bum reduced to cleaning the offal from the slum houses he once owned. His degeneration has also been marked by attacks of lycanthropy, during which he pads around the floor on all fours, naked, howling like a wolf. His only true friend—a man curiously named Dolly—becomes the unconvincingly innocent prey of venereal disease; his false friend Geary manages to acquire most of Vandover's property.

Rarely has virtue been so fictionally frustrated, but putting together this story probably had a therapeutic effect on Norris by enabling him to get grievances out of his system that might have prevented his doing justice to *McTeague*. The very act of writing *Vandover* could have given him the confidence in his own capacity for self-discipline and productive work that would allow him to turn his critical eye on some of the shortcomings of society that he had glanced at only in passing in his first long work.

The moral of this novel is not self-apparent, however, because even when we recognize that the present version does not represent the author's final intentions, we must deal with some internal problems before we can fairly consider the "message." In the first place, even though Charles Norris speaks of a "completed manuscript" being found in a trunk that had been removed from a warehouse in time to escape destruction by the San Francisco fire, he is reputed to have added five thousand words before the work was published. He did not specify where he made the additions or why. I believe, however, that there is evidence in the first two chapters of a hand besides the original author's.

I was never conscious of how completely different the first two chapters are from the rest of the novel until preparing this present study. I was startled to discover that I had voluminous notes on these opening chapters, comparatively few on subsequent ones. Re-examining the chapters, I found that the first two were as heavy with "significant statements" as a textbook, but that they were neither very vividly worded nor dramatically effective. The difference between them and the succeeding chapters can be explained by some of Frank Norris' own observations about novel writing.

Discussing the difference between the skillful and unskillful storyteller in "Simplicity in Art," he writes:

> The unskillful story-teller as often as not tells the story to himself as well as to his hearers as he goes along. Not sure of exactly how he is to reach the end, not sure even of the end itself, he must feel his way from incident to incident, from page to page, fumbling, using many words, repeating himself. . . .
> But in master works of narrative there is none of this shamming, no shoddyism, no humbug. . . . Comment is superfluous. If the author makes the scene appear terrible to the reader he need not say to himself or in the mouth of some protagonist, "It is terrible!" (VII, 188).

The meaning of the incidents, he maintains, should be conveyed metaphorically through them, not through the author's editorializing. The reader should react directly to the event, not to the author's comments on it. In the first two chapters of *Vandover,* the reader is told what the incidents mean; in most of the rest of the book, he is obliged to find out for himself.

The artistic shortcomings of the opening chapters might, of course, be attributable simply to the author's inexperience, but even such slight early stories as "Travis Hallett's Half-Back" show that Norris was already skilled in making events speak for themselves. The weakness of the first two chapters is precisely the one that critics have most often objected to in Charles Norris' own overtly tractarian novels—the failure or inability to let the incidents speak for themselves. Since Norris' brother admits to having made additions to the novel, he is most likely to have been responsible for those parts that most resemble his own writing.

The first two chapters also differ from the rest in that they contain fairly little dialogue, while the rest of the book—particularly the other early chapters in which the background for the major events is being presented—are largely conversational. There is also a marked difference in the style. We observe, for example, two passages from different parts of the book in which the writer is trying to make the same distinction, the first from Chapter XIII and the second from Chapter II:

> In the wreckage of all that was good that had been going on in him his love for all art was yet intact. It was the strongest side of his nature and it would be the last to go (V, 182).

> The brute had grown larger in him, but he knew that he had the creature in hand. He was its master, and only on rare occasions did he permit himself to gratify its demands, feeding its abominable hunger from that part of him which he knew to be the purest, the cleanest, and the best (V, 25).

The process described in the first quotation is entirely clear— the brute has infected all but Vandover's best part; the second quotation is unintelligible since one could not feed an internal hunger from one's best part without diminishing or sullying that part. The passage would have some meaning in itself and in the context of the rest of the novel if it said that some concessions from less vital parts were made to appease the brute hunger and at the same time protect and preserve the best part. The second quotation, however, is just what a diligent but insensitive repairman might make of someone else's illegible or unintelligible notes.

I dwell this long on the problem of the first two chapters because interpretation of the book is simplified if they are not really Frank Norris' work. One reason that eliminating them from consideration is helpful is that they really add nothing essential to the narrative. The novel is a more satisfying artistic entity without them, and Frank Norris may well have left them unfinished because he was still groping for the best way to begin the story when he laid it aside.[1]

A problem besides that posed by Charles Norris' unexplained additions concerns Vandover's lycanthropy, which is responsible for some of the most vivid scenes in the book. Although the outbreaks of the affliction attract attention, they really contribute nothing essential to making the author's point. Whether these passages would have remained in a revised version of the book, except to provide a grotesque external symbol of Vandover's internal state, cannot be known; but the use of this sensational material seems to be a hangover from the Gothicism of *Yvernelle* and "Lauth" and to be evidence of the artist's immaturity.

The reason for considering the lycanthropic displays non-essential is that—as Ernest Marchand points out—they are apparently the result of a nervous disorder and not moral obliquity. If Norris is suggesting that the disease is a punishment for Vandover's wickedness, he is writing more under the influence of Cotton Mather than Emile Zola; if, on the other hand, the disease is not a punishment, Norris obscures the serious psychological issues he raises for the sake of a sensational effect. From a dramatic viewpoint, the lycanthropy would be more shocking if it were visited upon an otherwise entirely innocent person—as venereal disease is upon Vandover's virtuous friend Dolly Haight. Since Norris had apparently not decided whether he was writing an ironic deterministic novel or a cautionary tale when he introduced the lycanthropy, the outbreaks of the disease actually weaken rather than strengthen both the symbolic value of Vandover and the moral effectiveness of the tale.

The young author, however, probably could not resist the bizarre device, since it afforded him a justification for having his hero rip off his clothes and go down on all fours in a graphic demonstration of the beast he had become. Norris evidently enjoyed writing sensational scenes like the one in which Vandover's drunken friends importune him to put on his "dog act," but there is no evidence that he understood enough about the nervous disorder to present a serious study of it. We can accuse Norris here of simply exploiting a pathological condition in order to produce "thrills," something that he also did in such a distressing short story as "The Dis-Associated Charities."

The novel is inadequate not only as a study of lycanthropy but even as the warning against self-indulgence which Norris keeps pointing out he intended it to be. That the story got out of his control—in ways other than his brother and H. L. Mencken suspected[2]—is apparent from the way in which the later chapters also violate Norris' principles of letting the incidents speak for themselves. An affinity to nineteenth-century tractarians is especially apparent if we compare these passages:

> He clearly saw the fate toward which he was hurrying; it was not too late to save himself if he only could find help, but he could find *no* help. His terror increased almost to hysteria.

It was one of those dreadful moments that men sometimes undergo that must be met alone . . . a glimpse that does not come often lest the reason brought to the edge of the fearful gulf should grow dizzy at the sight, and reeling, topple headlong.

. . . .

He loved his mother, and was deeply afflicted by the calamity; but it seemed as if he could not stop. Some terrible necessity appeared to be impelling him onward. If he formed good resolutions— and I doubt not that he did—they were blown away like threads of gossamer, the moment he came within the sphere of old associations.

The first of these is from *Vandover* (V, 192), but the second is from the holy writ of the temperance movement, *Ten Nights in a Bar-Room* by T. S. Arthur. Nor is it likely that the first passage can be charged to Charles Norris, since it is repeated almost verbatim in *A Man's Woman* (VI, 121). The style here, furthermore, is melodramatic, not pedantic as in the first two chapters of the novel.

Norris also strains too hard to keep the reader from confusing the author's interpretation of Vandover's plight with the character's own:

[Vandover] wondered at himself because of the quickness with which he recovered from this grief. . . . Could it be true, that nothing affected him very deeply? Was his nature shallow?

However, he was wrong in this respect; his nature was not shallow. It had merely become deteriorated (V, 138-39).

Norris maintains that self-indulgence has been Vandover's undoing; but I hold that the explanations he provided for both himself and his character fail to account adequately for Vandover's decline and that a third is more satisfactory when we do let the incidents speak for themselves, although the author—like many naïve storytellers—may not have been conscious of the pattern discernible in the events.

When we first meet Vandover, we are apparently expected to think highly of him because he has artistic talent and respects women and his elders. Since neither of these characteristics is evidence of any great intellectual depth, however, the man appears—whatever the author may have intended—a kind of carefree, cheerful lout. His troubles begin when his seduction—on a moment's impulse—of another bumpkin leads to the girl's and his father's deaths. As the passage quoted above shows, Vandover is not very much moved by either event. Offhand, one is inclined to agree with his own judgment that he is shallow rather than with the author's since Norris has failed to prove that Vandover had started at a point of development from which he could degenerate very much. Yet even shallowness is not quite the right word. Over and over Vandover displays characteristics of another failing.

Ida's seduction, as already pointed out, was not maliciously planned but simply happened one night when conditions were right. The death of his father actually irritates Vandover more than it grieves him, because it obliges him to manage his own affairs for the first time. He is conspicuously unsuccessful. He soon gives up the handling of matters that might provide him with a satisfactory income:

> By the end of three weeks Vandover had sickened of the whole thing. The novelty was gone, and business affairs no longer amused him. . . . Little by little [he] turned over the supervision and management of his affairs to Adams & Brunt, declaring that he could not afford to be bothered with them any longer. This course was much more expensive . . . but Vandover felt as though the loss in money was more than off-set by his freedom from annoyance and responsibility (V, 147-48).

Yet he uses his free time, for example, to spend two days twisting and rolling paper "lights" to be used in place of matches. When he must choose between two apartments, he is "undecided whether he should sacrifice his studio for his sitting-room, or his sitting-room for his studio." Although he concludes that to an artist "a good studio is the first consideration," he finally chooses the comfort of the good sitting room, where he fritters away his time "rearranging the smaller ornaments, adjusting the calendar, winding the clock, and, above all, tending the famous tiled stove" (V, 152-58). Later when he is sued by the father of the girl he seduced, because he is "sick of everything" and anxious to settle the complicated matter in one day, he allows his "friend" Geary to gain control of a valuable piece of property (V, 231). Still later he is put out of his luxurious apartment and loses his treasured furnishings because "almost before he knew it he

owed for six months' room and board," and is "confused" by the
bill he cannot believe and the figures he cannot understand
(V, 238). When he does acquire some money that he might
use to recover his furniture, he falls into the habit of gambling
and eventually squanders his whole fortune. When he receives
a notice from the bank that his account is overdrawn, he does
not "see the meaning." Norris explains:

> From time to time his bank-book had been balanced, and in-
> variably during the first days of each month his checks had come
> back to him, used and crumpled, covered with strange signatures
> and stamped in blue ink; but after the first few months he had
> never paid the least attention to these; he never kept accounts,
> having a veritable feminine horror of figures (V, 260).

What all this adds up to is not simply self-indulgence, but an
inability to cope with the practical problems of living in an urban
society and to accept the responsibilities of mature man in a
civilized state. Vandover's trouble is not that he degenerates, but
that he fails to grow.

Norris' blind spot is obviously his notion of "natural goodness." He is far more convincing when he depicts Vandover
shirking his responsibilities than when he depicts him "losing"
his ability to paint ("The forms he made on the canvas were no
adequate reflection of those in his brain . . . [but] he knew that
it was not because his hand lacked cunning on account of long
disuse" V, 196-97). That Norris' thinking is still traditionally
moralistic and not at all deterministic is evident from his failure
even to consider that Vandover's self-indulgence was a result
of his frustration rather than that his frustration was a punishment for self-indulgence. The author confused the symptom with
the disease—as he was bound to do if he accepted a notion of
the child as being "purer" than the man, since it precluded his
seeing the advantages of growing up intellectually.

The end of the novel justifies its interpretation as a lament
for lost childhood, but even here Norris' penchant for the sensational is likely to distract the reader's attention from what is
important. We are likely to be so shocked at the end of the
story to find the allegedly once sensitive artist reduced to cleaning a moldy hambone and other offal from beneath a kitchen
sink in a workman's filthy house, that we may not notice that
the book does not end with this nauseating incident, but with the

defeated Vandover looking into the eyes of a little boy "standing before him eating the last mouthful of his bread and butter" (V, 311). Norris refrains from comment upon this tableau, but the poignant contrast he draws between the innocence of the child and the degradation of the adult is inescapable. If only one did not have to grow up into such a dirty world!

When we recognize that a Peter Pan complex colors this scene, we may also understand why two subplots in the novel make Norris' moral purpose somewhat inscrutable. Although Vandover is apparently punished for the wickedness of self-indulgence, the entirely virtuous Dolly Haight suffers terribly through no fault of his own, while Geary, who betrays and swindles his friends, goes unpunished. If we consider these characters in isolation, the novel does seem a straight deterministic fable about an indifferent universe; but how can these subplots be reconciled with the puritanical morality of the main story?

The three fit together only if the novel is considered—intentionally or not—as an attack upon urban civilization. The evils of city life afflict not only the guilty Vandover, but also the innocent and significantly named Dolly, neither of whom can adjust himself to its amorality; while Geary (a mechanistic name?) is able to triumph because he understands the complex technicalities of commercial civilization and knows how to use them to his own advantage. The city, in Norris' work, as in the fulminations of many of his eighteenth- and nineteenth-century predecessors, is an unnatural place where the innocent suffer, the susceptible go astray, and the corrupt flourish. Those who are not adept in its unnatural ways are destroyed. Virtue means nothing here; the prize goes to the technically competent. We might wonder how much of the war between science and religion may have been prompted by the faithfuls' terror of science's demanding techniques and the inutility of merely moral stature in acquiring them.

Actually Norris buries what proves to be the real moral of his story in the middle of the book. At the end of the fourteenth chapter, he writes:

> It was Life, the murmur of the great, mysterious force that spun the wheels of Nature and that sent it onward like some enormous engine, resistless, relentless; an engine that sped straight forward, driving before it the infinite herd of humanity, driving it on at breathless speed through all eternity, driving

it no one knew whither, *crushing out inexorably all those who lagged behind the herd* and who fell from exhaustion, grinding them to dust, beneath its myriad iron wheels . . . (V, 202; italics mine).

Vandover was one who lagged behind the herd; despite Norris' moralizing it is not really Vandover who is the culprit, but as in *An American Tragedy* an order of things (though not as definite a social order as in Dreiser's novel) that places people in situations they are incapable of handling. The culprit in *Vandover* is a technological civilization which, instead of suppressing the brute, indifferently allows it to triumph over virtue. *Vandover* is not the only work of Norris' in which the culprit is thus identified.[3]

CHAPTER *4*

The Gilded Cage

DESPITE SUPERFICIAL differences resulting largely from the different economic classes portrayed, *Vandover* and *McTeague* (probably written from 1894 to 1896 but published in 1899) are remarkably similar. Both depict in lurid detail the degeneration of a strapping specimen of manhood incapable of coping with the intellectual complexities of urban civilization. The author's preoccupation with decay in both works is in striking contrast to his excited affirmation in *The Octopus* of forces working inevitably toward goodness—although he may have changed only his tactics not his mind. The Hoovens in *The Octopus* suffer in the same way as McTeague, but the later novel allows the last word to the character who rejects rather than succumbs to civilization.

When he wrote *McTeague*, Norris was still content to employ the time-tried tractarian method of the "horrible example" story. Not since the 1840's had seen a wave of books about the "Mysteries" of New York, Philadelphia, Fitchburg and other such centers of depravity had the pitfalls of the metropolis been so grimly presented. Poor McTeague (we never learn his first name) should have stayed at the mines, but his mother had ambitions for him. He learned his trade from an itinerant dentist and settled in San Francisco, where we first meet him practicing without a license. All goes well until he falls in love with his best friend's cousin, Trina Sieppe. Even then life might have continued tranquilly had not Trina won five thousand dollars in a lottery. This windfall brings out her miserly instincts and makes the cousin—who had thought of marrying her himself—feel that he has been cheated. He reports McTeague for practicing without a license. When McTeague is obliged to give up dentistry, he cannot find another job he can hold and Trina refuses to spend either her winnings or the interest they earn.

The couple degenerates. McTeague steals some of Trina's money and deserts her; and, after she loses a hand as a result of his brutality, she becomes a charwoman. Her miserly instincts so overpower her that she finally withdraws her money from her uncle's firm in which it is invested and keeps it about her in gold pieces. Sunk to poverty, McTeague breaks in on her one night, kills her, and steals the gold. He flees into the mountains but is pursued by Marcus. The novel comes to a sensational conclusion on the blazing sands of Death Valley; McTeague is out of water and is handcuffed to the body of Marcus, whom he has also murdered.

This tale that most of Norris' contemporaries found repulsive is counterpointed by two subplots. One concerns Zerkow, an avaricious Jewish junk dealer, who marries a mad charwoman and murders her in hopes of acquiring an imaginary gold dinner service; the other describes the painfully slow process by which two gentle and affectionate old people who live in adjoining rooms finally become acquainted and marry. These two couples provide bad and good examples from which McTeague and Trina could have learned—but did not. A final character is a canary that accompanies McTeague throughout his adventures and testifies that the man did have "a heart of gold" that might have triumphed had not others been distracted by the more obvious glitter of golden coins.

From the viewpoint of the kind of "indirect" artistry Norris admired, *McTeague* is a considerable advance over *Vandover*, for the author avoids comments and allows the characters to speak—often rather shrilly—for themselves. As a well-designed work of art, however, *McTeague* leaves much to be desired, for either Norris' structural ability or his patience flagged early. After having started to build a mosaic-like novel in which every incident fit specifically into an over-all design, he lapsed into the loose form of the episodic novel and devised a series of vivid but loosely connected "acts" that much resemble the vaudeville show described with affectionate enthusiasm in the novel.

What Norris might have accomplished had his taste run to the "well-made" play, or had he been as conscious of over-all design as James or Conrad, is illustrated by the first four chapters of the novel which display an intricate structure that has not been sufficiently analyzed or praised. In these chapters, form and meaning are interrelated in a way that provides clues to the meaning of the novel as a whole and that can be gleaned only with much greater difficulty from the later, loosely assembled chapters.

The first chapter characterizes McTeague's heredity and environment. He is presented as sluggish, unambitious, easily pleased, and hopelessly stupid—a combination of qualities which makes it difficult for him to control situations or even to respond appropriately to changes in them. McTeague is surely no irresistible conqueror; and, although most contemporary and later criticisms of the novel were directed against its vulgarity and brutality, we wonder if its offensiveness may not have resulted principally from readers' violent rejection of a character who so completely violated the American dream of the young man "making his way" in the world. Norris contradicted not only that spinner of popular dreams Horatio Alger, but the guardians of the genteel tradition—Howells and James, who in *A Hazard of New Fortunes* and *The Bostonians* had paid tribute to intellectual frontiersmen.

A large part of the opening chapter of *McTeague* is devoted to a description of the daily round of life on Polk Street, a neighborhood shopping artery. Dismissing this material as simply providing background for the action is a mistake. Norris does not merely insert the description as a historical novelist might; he integrates it into the characterization of his protagonist when he stresses that "Day after day, McTeague saw the *same* panorama unroll itself. The bay window of his 'Dental Parlours' was for him a point of vantage from which he watched the world go past" (VII, 7; italics mine).

The routine of Polk Street is a source of McTeague's security, and in identifying himself with it—participating vicariously through his window—he identifies himself with an unconscious rhythm of life. A stable oasis in a turbulent world, Polk Street is a kind of run-down Eden, in which the "natural," unthinking man can flourish. The first chapter presents us with a world where the individual and his surroundings are harmoniously related. The arrangement is too good to last, and even before the end of the chapter a brace of serpents violates the Garden.

The first is Marcus Schouler, who eventually destroys McTeague's world. Interestingly enough, the diabolical Marcus is introduced as a man who thinks—or at least tries to—about "issues":

He was continually making use of the stock phrases of the professional politicians—phrases he had caught at some of the ward "rallies" and "ratification meetings." These rolled off his tongue with incredible emphasis, appearing at every turn of the conversation—"outraged constituencies," "cause of labor," "wage earners," "Opinions biased by personal interest," "eyes blinded by party prejudice" (VIII, 11).

Norris could simply be foreshadowing the Southern Agrarians in satirizing the pretentiousness of the lower classes in displaying political interests, but Marcus may be not so much a symbol of a particular class as of the type of person who is more interested in parroting abstract principles than in enjoying the routine of everyday living, who "thinks" rather than "feels." This passage suggests why Norris did not actively associate himself with any of the reform parties of his period. It also leads us to sympathize with McTeague, who understands not a word of such talks but cares for his canary.

The second serpent to appear—although in this chapter only in conversation—is Trina. With the casual mention of her coming to McTeague's dental parlors, the stage is set for the hero's eventual downfall.

The next three chapters constitute an extraordinarily well-organized and carefully balanced unit. The second opens with a description of Miss Baker and Old Grannis, the elderly people who live in adjoining rooms and long to meet, but who are too shy to speak to each other. Both are thrilled to discover that the wallpaper of one's room continues into the other's, since this discovery leads them to believe that at one time it was "all one room," so that "it almost amounts to our occupying the same room" (VIII, 16)—as Norris might have presumed all people did when they lived "naturally." The fourth chapter closes with a description of two dogs who live on opposite sides of a "thin, board fence" and rage at each other, "snarling and barking, frantic with hate" (VIII, 53).

The group of chapters is thus framed by accounts of two ways in which "unnatural" partitions separate individuals. The "romance" between Miss Baker and Old Grannis has often been unjustly objected to as only a kind of "comic relief" for the sordid story of McTeague and Trina, but as William B. Dillingham shows in "The Old Folks of *McTeague*" (*Nineteenth-*

Century Fiction, September, 1961) this subplot, through an elaborate series of contrasts, serves actually to balance and counterpoint the main story. The tale of the old folks provides not only a welcome note of optimism in a generally grim book, but it also contributes another proof of the degenerate artificiality of the city, which not only brings together those who will destroy each other, but separates those who belong together. In contrast to the opening description of McTeague and the "natural" rhythm of Polk Street life, both the vignettes of the romantic old people and of the snarling beasts exemplify the way in which civilization builds barriers that keep "Nature" from exercising its benign influence.

Ultimately both barriers prove to have fostered false illusions. Although the human characters have supposed that the snarling dogs would fight if they ever met, when they do meet they refuse, with "the dignity of monarchs," to battle (VIII, 185-86). When after long years of loneliness, Old Grannis and Miss Baker are finally brought together—partly as a result of the abortive dog fight—each learns that the other has been longing to cross the polite barrier that separated them and, in the most sentimental chapter in the novel, they enter upon "the long retarded romance of their commonplace and uneventful lives" (VIII, 280). Thus civilization breeds misconceptions.

The remainder of the second and fourth chapters are devoted to a paired presentation of McTeague's triumph over his brute instinct to take advantage of the defenseless Trina while she is unconscious in his dental chair, and of Marcus' renunciation of his interest in the girl when he hears of his friend's infatuation. Both of these appear to be illustrations of the benign influences of civilization—the conquest of lust by a sense of responsibility and the surrender of selfish desires to serve a friend—that bode well for the future.

Between these two incidents, however, Norris inserts the vastly different third chapter, in which for the first time we hear Maria, the mad charwoman, describe to Zerkow the fantastic gold dinner service her Guatemalan family allegedly possesses and see his greedy response to her description. Placing this picture of unrestrained passions excited by a symbol of elegance and wealth between two chapters depicting the self-imposed restraints of civilized society sets up a tension between gentility and brutality that underlies the whole novel. If Norris had continued building on the foundation that he laid in these chapters, he might have produced a remarkably well-balanced, dramatic study of the competing forces of self-indulgence and self-restraint that might rate comparison with Faulkner's *Light in August.*

The artistry, however, begins to deteriorate in the fifth chapter in which the symbolism becomes too obvious. Early in the chapter Trina's excruciatingly methodical father's inability to operate a mechanical toy boat results in the toy's sinking on its trial run and foreshadows what will happen to the family when he matches wits with the mechanized civilization that produced the boat; but the episode is a digression since it is not essential— like those in the previous chapters—to establish the character of the principals. The famous springing of the mousetrap at the end of the chapter, when Trina's mother learns of the girl's feeling for McTeague, is simply gratuitous theatricality. It arrests attention, but it fails to symbolize anything relevant to the story since the mousetrap is much too civilized an artifact to serve as an emblem of the unsophisticated Sieppes. They do not ensnare McTeague; rather both he and they are trapped by conditions they do not understand. Norris, however, never learned enough artistic self-restraint to resist the employment, when they occurred to him, of the catchpenny devices that he had reveled in when writing claptrap like "The Jongleur of Taillebois."

Indeed—as Ernest Marchand shows in detail—the only unifying symbols employed consistently throughout the novel are the numerous golden objects: the five thousand dollars in twenty-dollar gold pieces that is the undoing of Trina; the golden tooth that symbolizes McTeague's professional success and that Norris once thought of using to provide a title for the novel; the imaginary golden dinner service that is Maria's undoing; the canary bird in its gilt cage. All of these serve not only, as Marchand points out, as material tokens of the greed which destroys the characters,[1] but also as emblems of the ostentatious, superficial age in which Norris had grown up and which Mark Twain had well denominated "Gilded." Yet after McTeague murders Trina —the incident with which a truly naturalistic novel would most appropriately end—even these symbols are not effectively managed. Norris was not yet sufficiently critical of himself to realize as much about conveying his meaning through symbol and structure as well as through language as he would know when he began the Wheat trilogy. The symbols embellish rather than tell the story.

After the murder of Trina drives McTeague from San Francisco and he begins to display a mysterious "sixth sense" of being pursued, the novel becomes straight Gothicism. Its lurid final tableau has been hailed as an imaginative triumph (even Norris himself defended it against Howells' criticism), but to discover that it exhibits only that penchant for sensationalism that enabled many a deft romancer to produce prolifically such blood-curdling ironies, we need simply recall the closing moments of *Il Trovatore* or many of Verdi's other operas.

This conclusion also shows how extremely moralistic the book really is. A thoroughly naturalistic writer—having already made his point about McTeague's deterioration—would not have cared whether he was punished or not and so would probably simply have ended the story with his flight from Polk Street after murdering Trina.

As art *McTeague* leaves much to be desired. The novel is not likely to excite much enthusiasm among critics who cherish formal perfection, although the very unevenness of the technique enables us to discover much about the author's state of mind.

What has most attracted readers to *McTeague*, however is caught in the title of Erich Von Stroheim's remarkable motion-picture version—*Greed*. As a denunciation of the evils of the lust for gold, the initial impact of the novel is tremendous. The scenes of the barroom brawl between McTeague and Marcus, the discovery of Maria's corpse, and the perverted behavior of Trina with her twenty-dollar gold pieces are the kind that allow the novel to share something of the tremendous immediacy of the motion picture. Theodore Dreiser correctly appraised the novel (excepting its conclusion) when he wrote that "no book, before or since . . . is essentially more correct as to milieu or situations" (VIII, xi).

Norris' kinship with the tractarians is nowhere more apparent than in his technique in *McTeague* of piling horrible example upon horrible example to present a case without a word of direct preaching. If people are saved from the bottle by temperance tracts, I cannot see how the pathologically avaricious could look a gold piece in its glistening face after reading *McTeague*. Yet as a tract, too, the novel ultimately fails. It offended impressionable readers of its own time with its graphic descriptions of violence and squalor. Norris probably felt, of course, that his novel would be ignored if it were too conventionally tractarian, and so determined that it could not be confused with Sunday-school literature; but in so doing he cut himself off from the genteel custodians of morality who might have supported his efforts.

Paradoxically the objection of more "advanced" thinkers to *McTeague* as a tract is that it is simply old wine in new bottles—too traditional in its moralizing to merit later consideration as more than a museum piece. Some of the material—Trina's literally rolling in her wealth, the anti-Semitism in the portrayal of the junkman—a discriminating reader today must find either distressingly benighted or indefensibly silly. Although Norris deplored greed, he did not really know much about its causes. Attempting to explain Trina's motives, he comes up with nothing but: "Economy was her strong point. A good deal of peasant blood still ran undiluted in her veins, and she had all the instinct of a hardy and penurious mountain race—the instinct which saves without any thought, without idea of consequence—saving for the sake of saving, hoarding without knowing why" (VIII, 116-17).

Cultural anthropologists would be dismayed at the notion of "peasant blood," while psychologists would find the attribution of such behavior to "instinct" little more illuminating than Trina's own explanation when told that she is a miser, "I can't help it, and it's a good fault" (VIII, 214).

Norris' ideas of motivation are no advance over T. S. Arthur's, and as an analysis of *why* people behave as they do *McTeague* belongs on the shelf with *Ten Nights in a Bar-room*. Norris cannot, of course, be blamed for having been born into a pre-Freudian world whose easy attributions of evil to diabolical agencies or brute instincts were about to receive their death-blow; but an indication of the superficiality of the innovations which loom large in most accounts of his work is his easy acquiescence to the conventional thinking of his time on the most crucial problems of human behavior.

If McTeague is deficient as both art and morality, does it deserve its long continued success and the recent revival of interest in it? What accounts for the undeniable power of the novel that keeps us reading despite a growing annoyance with the novelist's intellectual limitations? The answer to the second question leads to the answer to the first. Norris has frequently—and entirely justifiably—been described as a great reporter; this tribute would be a small matter if great reporters were common, but they are not. As any conscientious composition teacher soon learns, the uncommonest writer is the one who can report what he sees or hears clearly, objectively, and economically so that the reader can visualize it just as it might appear to him rather than as obscured by a haze of prejudices and preconceptions. Most communications are fuzzy, garbled, and repetitious, because most people are engrossed not with the external world, but with the muddle in their own heads.

As this study suggests, there was muddle enough in Norris' head, but he managed to get something down on paper besides projections of his own neural patterns. He loved the world around him—especially San Francisco—enough to want to preserve it, so that he filled the "notebooks" that his brother Charles says were his greatest treasures with affectionately enthusiastic descriptions of the sights and sounds and smells of a fascinating city.

The greatness of *McTeague* lies in the description of the Polk Street routine, in the catalogue of the furnishings and even the odors of the McTeague apartment, in the chronicle of the orgiastic wedding dinner (boring novelists fail to recognize that strong sensory descriptions of what the characters are eating enable the reader to project himself into the story), in the details of the picnics at Schuetzen Park, and in the irrelevant yet absorbing account of the vaudeville program. The setting is not merely a group of backdrops against which the story unfolds; it shapes the story as much as it does in Hardy's novels, in which the psychology is often as dubious as the sense of the interrelation of individual and environment is unerring. What Norris has done in *McTeague* is to preserve the physical characteristics of an important era in human affairs—the period immediately before the electrification of the city established the distinctive quality of twentieth-century domestic life.

We today cannot imagine what life was like in the 1890's. Although city dwellers still live isolated from each other, electrical gadgets—especially radio and television, but also even central generating systems—have destroyed the possibility of the kind of intellectual isolation that characterized the inhabitants of Polk

Street in the days before everyone shared the same prefabricated fantasy world just by turning a switch. *McTeague* affords those who wish it a window upon the past through which they may observe the same kind of panorama as the dentist did.

But doesn't the superficiality and conventionality of Norris' thought counteract the value of the pictorial qualities of his work? Rather, I think, they enhance them by preserving something of the thinking as well as the appearance of his era. Norris' kinship to nineteenth-century moralists rather than twentieth-century psychologists is especially apparent in his oversimplified notions of motivation.

Let us consider, for example, the frequent interpretation of *McTeague* as an attack upon greed. When the novel is scrutinized closely, greed is not enough to account for all that happens. Certainly the junk dealer whose manic desire for a gold dinner service causes him to kill his wife when she no longer feeds his appetite for opulent fantasy exemplifies the stereotyped concept of avarice; but Norris weakens any universal symbolism by giving his lurid allegory anti-Semitic overtones.

Trina, however, who is offered as the major exhibit of the evils of greed, is quite another matter. As long as she merely scrimps on household expenditures, she seems conventionally parsimonious; but her increasing delight in the physical handling of gold pieces suggests that she is troubled by more than lustful acquisitiveness. When at last she withdraws the money that she has invested in her uncle's toy business and takes to little amusements like spreading "all the gold pieces between the sheets . . . stripping herself" and then sleeping "all night upon the money, taking a strange and ecstatic pleasure in the touch of the smooth flat pieces the length of her entire body" (VII, 306), we are dealing with behavior far more primitive than that usually evidencing greed—something that is actually a form of gluttony.

The greedy person might have withdrawn his money from one business in response to the lure of possibly higher returns elsewhere and might eventually have come to grief in the same way as those whose cupidity leads them into the hands of confidence men; but the kind of miserliness Trina displays is rather the result of a deep-seated fear of being deprived of something tangible that may lead people to overeat or even to collect bags full of worthless trash.

Explaining in *Language in Thought and Action,* the basis of certain forms of behavior, S. I. Hayakawa draws a useful distinction between what he calls "thing-handlers" and "symbol-handlers":

> Whenever people of a pre-monetary culture (farmers, fishermen, and other rural folk who live on what they produce . . .) come into contact with people skilled in money and credit transactions (those who understand bookkeeping, interest, mortgages, notes, banking, and such matters), the latter are likely to take advantage of the former. The former are *handlers of economic things* (potatoes, fish, coconuts) and the latter are *handlers of economic symbols* (notes, bills, futures, covering the exchange of potatoes, fish, coconuts). The thing-handlers, even if they have not been taken advantage of, are likely to feel suspicious and uneasy in dealings with the symbol-handlers. The former are not skilled in computing interest; many have difficulty with simple addition and subtraction; the words in the fine print of sales agreements and contracts are over their heads.[2]

McTeague is such a perfect example of the "thing handler" that Hayakawa could have drawn his definition from him. Trying to purchase theatre tickets, he is "bewildered, confused; misunderstood directions" (VIII, 81); he cannot understand investments and interest at all and can think of five thousand dollars only in the concrete terms of buying a house or furniture (VIII, 114). When he gets a position in Trina's uncle's shipping department that involves "a certain amount of ciphering," he is "obliged to throw it up in two days" (VIII, 258). His troubles are not only mathematical. Just as Vandover allowed himself to be talked out of his real estate, McTeague allows Maria to talk him out of some valuable dental instruments that simply need repair (VIII, 36), and he fails to understand a word of Marcus' anticapitalistic orations, responding only when Marcus calls his foes "white-livered drones," "Yes, . . I think it's their livers" (VIII, 12).

Although his mother's ambitions have caused him to gravitate to the city, McTeague remains a most primitive backwoodsman in his thought.[3] He has not even the most elementary understanding of how a commercial economy works; thus, as Richard Chase points out, he is "corrupted and defeated" by the "evil" city. The important thing, however, is that he and Trina are two of a kind. Although she hoards money and he flings it away, she is as completely "thing-oriented" in her thinking as he.

One evidence of her state of mind is her curious concept of investment. She finally decides to withdraw her money from her uncle's business after thinking in this manner:

> Trina told herself that she must have her money in hand. She longed to see again the heap of it upon her work-table where she could plunge her hands into it, her face into it, feeling the cool, smooth metal upon her cheeks. At such moments she would see in her imagination her wonderful five thousand dollars piled in columns, shining and gleaming somewhere at the bottom of Uncle Oelbermann's vault (VIII, 302).

Although she explains something about investment to Mc-Teague, she understands nothing of its principles herself. Significantly she works with her hands, making Noah's Ark animals, and when the family meets its most serious challenge she shows the "thing-handler's" almost hysterical fear of the "symbol-handler": "No, no, don't go near the law courts. *I* know them. The lawyers take all your money, and you lose your case. We're bad off as it is, without lawing about it" (VIII, 238).

A "thing-handler" may, of course, live inconspicuously and at peace in an urban community as long as no conflicts involving things and symbols arise between him and the community.[4] The real climax of *McTeague* occurs when such a conflict does arise—when, apparently as a result of Marcus' desire for revenge, McTeague's right to practice dentistry is challenged because despite his long experience (with things) he does not possess a diploma (which Norris, in view of his educational theories, would regard as only a symbol of technical proficiency). If the McTeagues had gone to court, his practice might have been preserved; but he, out of ignorance, and she, out of fear, succumb to the "thing-handler's" traditional fear of the "symbol-handler." After McTeague loses his right to practice, he begins to deteriorate and Trina becomes infatuated with the physical rather than the symbolic value of her gold coins.

Thus what we have here is really not so much an attack upon greed as another attack—like *Vandover and the Brute*—upon commercial civilization. Even Charles Hoffmann goes too far when he says that Trina and McTeague are defeated by their own follies.[5] They are victims of civilization, but a civilization that is evil not because it has defects but simply because it exists. Even Norris himself suggests once in the book that civilization— at least in the form of "genteel refinement"—is the culprit. He observes that the loss of McTeague's practice is especially de-moralizing because "Unfortunately, Trina had cultivated tastes in McTeague which now could not be gratified" (VIII, 243). While it is not clear whether Norris thinks that the McTeagues should never have become civilized or that society should allow them to keep what they have, the use of the word "unfortunately" in this context strongly suggests that the author hated "symbol-handling" civilization altogether, that he thought of it as a gilded cage imprisoning the innocent. The canary that accom-panies McTeague from the beginning to the end of the book and dies with him is not just his pet, but his alter ego.

Norris himself had adequate reason for hating "symbol-hand-lers." He had tremendous difficulty with abstractions. A friend reports that it was an inability to master mathematics that kept Norris from ever becoming a regular student and getting a degree from the University of California.[6] While the author was writing *The Pit*, George Moulson had a great problem getting him to understand the operation of the futures market.[7] Norris' sym-pathies would be aroused for the "thing-handler" victimized by the "symbol-handlers," although he was probably too uneasy about his own difficulty with abstract thinking to state the prob-lem underlying *McTeague* objectively. He really did not think that the advantages of civilization were enough to compensate for its disadvantages, but talk about "instincts" and the sub-merged brute enabled him to avoid facing squarely the un-pleasant questions posed by the changing demands of civilized society upon the individual.

An attack upon "symbol-handling" has extraordinary value as a period document, for McTeague, Trina, and Norris were far from alone in their difficulties in manipulating symbols. Indeed much of the history of this country and most of the rest of the world during the past century has been one of decreasing de-mand for "thing-handlers" and increasing need for "symbol-handlers." The steadily diminishing demand for unskilled work-ers and the shortage of mathematicians are only the most obvious signs of a widespread situation. The greatest weakness of contemporary education is not the failure to train enough people who are specifically engineers or physicists, but the failure to produce enough people who can cope with "symbols" rather than "things" in almost any field (including literary study, where there has been a noticeable shift from the kind of "literary history" that is simply a study of things that can be memorized to a "literary criticism" that emphasizes the interpretation of symbols.)

Norris has not been alone among our literary men in joining the attack upon "symbol-handlers." One of this century's amazing spectacles has been the anti-intellectualism of writers whose books could only be comprehensible to those with extensive intellectual training. Perhaps the most vehement has been Ezra Pound, whose incessant attacks upon "usury" illustrate the "thing-handler's" irascible suspicions of "symbol-handlers" and whose poem "Salutation" (about the fishermen being happier than the readers and the fish happier than the fishermen) says in ten lines what Norris is driving at all the way through *McTeague*.

Attacks upon commercial civilization, especially by those who would preserve its plumbing and reject most of its other features, are likely to seem wishful silliness; yet we could not expect to see a "thing-dominated" world pass without a strong rear-guard action. Norris is important because he wrote at a time when the forces were more equally matched than today.[8] His attack upon a symbol-dominated civilization is, probably unintentionally, as true to the thinking that dominated his time as his effective descriptions are to its appearance.

McTeague is not a great piece of literature if by that hard-to-define term we mean an eternally fresh book like *Pride and Prejudice* or *Moby Dick* whose author speaks to us across the years about the condition of our own times. It cannot be recommended for its insight into the basic human condition. Yet it tells of the tragedy of more than one man. Like those works that lament the defeat of the Confederacy, it is a memorial to a lost cause, mourning the passing of a temporary order of things. As a period piece in which a talented observer, who was sensitive to the physical and intellectual characteristics of his time and who shared its fears and prejudices, brings to life the external and internal feelings of an age well symbolized by a wild bird imprisoned in a gilded cage, *McTeague* is distinguished by its author's fulfillment of his burning desire to tell the truth—by telling more of it than he realized.

CHAPTER *5*

Victorian Valkyries

I *Lady From The Sea*

ALTHOUGH *Vandover and the Brute* and *McTeague* had been written earlier, the first novel of Norris' to be published was *Moran of the Lady Letty* (1898). This adolescent fantasy was serialized in the *Wave* and won the author an editorial position on *McClure's Magazine* in New York and the friendship of some critics like Isaac Marcosson. The warmth of this reception indicates the abysmally bad quality of most popular literature in the 1890's. As either art or morality, *Moran* has no redeeming virtue; even the most naïve and depraved of the current television serials compares favorably with it. We would not even pause over the novel if it did not pose several serious questions about its author. The most obvious of these is whether or not a man willing to sign his name to such a display of sadism be taken seriously at all. Since there is no reason why most readers should disinter the novel, a brief summary will help clarify the answer.

Moran follows one Ross Wilbur, Yale man and athletic scion of a prominent San Francisco family, from the time he is brutally shanghaied until he returns a "nine-days-wonder" to his effete society. The story could have been ended quickly if Ross—once he had shaken off the effect of knockout drops—had elected to swim the hundred yards that separated him from some friends' yacht, but he finds that he is "enjoying himself" too much slumming nautically. After a number of improbable adventures, Ross joins forces with a shipwrecked girl, the Moran of the title, who is "not made for men." Although the doting Wilbur thinks she possesses "the purity of primeval glaciers," her philosophy is: "The strongest of us are going to live, and the weakest are going to die. I'm going to live and I'm going to have my loot, too" (III, 273).

Although Ross refuses to take advantage of her "innocence,"

because—he assures himself—he is "a thoroughbred, after all," he does not mind in the least giving her a vicious and minutely described beating, following which she announces that he has conquered her and she "loves" him for it. They plan to turn their backs on society and go filibustering in Cuba, but Moran is murdered in her bed by a thieving Chinese coolie, who steals the ambergris that was to support the couple's thumbing their nose at civilization.

I cannot say what a psychiatrist would make of this—especially the obvious relish with which the author describes a man beating up a woman instead of sleeping with her; Juliet Wilbor Tompkins says this scene inspired Norris to write the book.[1] It seems certain, however, that Norris supposed the tale would please the masses. The appeal he hoped to use in winning popular favor is evident from his early attempt to bring the reader into the story through the observation that "somewhere deep down in the heart of every Anglo-Saxon lies the predatory instinct of his Viking ancestors—an instinct that a thousand years of respectability and tax paying have not quite succeeded in eliminating" (III, 214). To the average reader's credit, this blatant appeal to racial snobbery and atavism has never lifted even into the ranks of popular "adventure" classics.

Whether Norris was sincere or cynical in writing a story based on such an appeal (and his motives were probably mixed), his thinking was obviously either too uninformed or too meretricious to be taken seriously. We have already observed that much of the value of Norris' work is accidental; his conscious thoughts are sometimes confused, but the events in his stories provide evidence of unconscious attitudes important to an understanding of American cultural history. The writer who can give form to such fierce fantasies cannot be considered a constructive thinker, but he may merit attention as one adhering to influential social theories so deeply and firmly entrenched that he is not consciously aware of them.

The most interesting problem about *Moran* is posed by its ending. Norris wrote Mrs. Elizabeth Davenport on March 12, 1898, "I am of two minds about [Moran] and do not know whether she should be killed or go to Cuba with Wilbur."[2] Why did he finally decide that she must die? Obviously the ending would not be popular with a public that likes even the goriest narratives to wind up with the hero and heroine riding off into the traditionally orgiastic sunset. Possibly Norris did not wish to go all the way in pandering to public taste and thought that he could maintain his artistic integrity and even educate the public's tragic sense by choosing the "unhappy" ending. It is also possible that he could not stand to think of this woman whom he twice calls a "Valkyrie," despoiled and reduced to the mediocrity of "normal" life. Norris implies that she has achieved a kind of Wagnerian resignation since, although she could easily have bested her attacker with a leg wrenched from her table, she refuses even to fight; her capitulation to Wilbur has made her "dependent."

These hypotheses are not mutually exclusive and can be reconciled with the most likely of all. Although Norris lavished adjectives like "savage, unconquered, untamed" upon Moran, he actually describes her best in a sentence he has her declaim: "I've lived by doing things, not by thinking things, or reading about what other people have done or thought; I guess it's what you do that counts, rather than what you think or read about" (III, 234). She is, like McTeague and Trina, a "thing-handler" rather than a "symbol-handler"; she is, as surely as they, what she is called in the book—"a creature unfit for civilization."

The destruction of this child of the sea, then, is another triumph of degenerate civilization over those who live in a harmonious relationship with a mysterious, primitive rhythm of Nature, with which Vanamee in *The Octopus* is able to re-establish contact. Moran's murder by a debased creature seeking to steal a fortune is another denunciation of the corrupting influence of civilization. If Ross Wilbur had actually won Moran, Norris would have compromised not only with the tradition of sentimental romance but also with the debilitating forces of a money-minded civilization. The author's difficulty in ending the novel suggests that he was both attracted and repulsed by the values represented by socialite Ross Wilbur and the ambergris; his choosing the tragic ending is most completely accounted for by considering a hatred of "unnatural" civilization as his strongest impulse.

II Refugee From The "Right" Set

In the middle period of his brief literary career, Norris produced three lightly regarded romances named for their tall, light-haired, mannish heroines. The second, *Blix* (1899), has been generally neglected by the critics, but slighting it is a serious mistake, comparable to ignoring *Die Meistersinger* when studying Wagner, because as the only truly light-hearted comedy among Norris' longer works, this Golden Gate pastoral is unique and important.

Blix is central to understanding Norris, because it offers his only positive picture of what a rightly functioning world would be like to contrast with the views of a world gone awry in *Vandover, McTeague, Moran,* and *The Octopus.* It concerns Travis Bessemer, young girl nicknamed "Blix," who breaks with smart but decadent San Francisco society, and her "chum" Condy Rivers, a young newspaperman with literary ambitions. Blix insists that Condy stop flirting with her and that they explore the city together as friends. Among other mild adventures, they arrange a marriage between a middle-aged lighthousekeeper and a genteel serving girl. By a stratagem, Blix also breaks Condy of his bad habit of gambling and provides him with enough money to take a month off to write a story based on one of the light-housekeeper's tales. As Blix is about to leave for medical school in New York, she and Condy discover they are truly in love; and his brief despair about his inability to go with her ends when a New York magazine publisher rejects Condy's story but offers him a job.

If Norris really believed that man at his best unconsciously acts in harmony with the rhythm of nature from which civilization alienates him, we should find somewhere in this most idyllic of his novels a statement of the way in which its principals achieve real happiness after renouncing conventionality by responding unthinkingly to the physical world about them—and indeed we do find such a statement. A long passage immediately preceding Condy's discovery that he truly loves Blix must be quoted because of the contrast it affords with statements about related points in Norris' pictures of society's seamy side:

> The simple things of the world, the great, broad, primal emotions of the race stirred in them. As they swung along, going toward the ocean, their brains were almost as empty of thought or of reflection as those of two fine, clean animals. They were all for the immediate sensation; they did not think—they felt. The intellect was dormant; they looked at things, they heard things, they smelt the smell of the sea and of the seaweed. . . . It was good to be alive on the royal morning. Just to be young was an

exhilaration; and everything was young with them—the day was young, the country was young, and the civilization to which they belonged, teeming there upon the green, Western fringe of the continent, was young and heady and tumultuous with the boisterous, red blood of a new race (III, 123).

Blix contains more, however, than just this wordy tribute to empty-headedness. Although no violence occurs, so that critics have been misled by its placidity, the novel describes a revolution; and from this description we can reconstruct the world Norris despised and learn what he thought should replace it. When it has been noticed at all, *Blix* has usually been read as autobiographical, and even Norris admitted parallels between his hero's life and his own; but making assumptions about Norris' behavior on the basis of the novel is unsound, since there are important discrepancies even in easily observed matters (Norris' father was not, like Condy's, dead, nor was Norris an only child.) While one should not assume that the novel retells the story of its author's life, it can be safely read as his spiritual autobiography. It describes not the life he lived, but the life he thought should be lived.

The manifesto of Blix's successful rebellion against elegant society emphasizes the necessity for utter sincerity. She revolts principally against the endless round of "functions" that she is expected to attend and the rules of decorum she is supposed to follow while attending them. Her rebellion against "playing the game" occurs after she is obliged to dance with a drunk at an elaborate party. She tells Condy:

> "I simply don't want to know the kind of people who have made Jack Carter possible . . . and I'm not going to be associated with people who take it as a joke for a man to come to a function drunk. And as for having a good time, I'll find my amusement somewhere else. . . . If the kind of thing that makes Jack Carter possible is conventionality, then I'm done with conventionality for good. I am going to try, from this time on, to be just as true to myself as I can be. . . . I'm going to do the things I like to do—just so long as they are the things a good girl can do" (III, 18-19).[3]

Norris' idea of how people should behave is projected through his picture of the activities Blix substitutes for the detested conventional "functions." She enjoys discovering San Francisco.

With Condy she braves a Chinese restaurant and resolves that she will often "go round to queer little, interesting little places." She even discovers that fishing is "better than teas, and dancing, and functions" (III, 76). Having definitely given up any intentions of "coming out," she resolves instead to do something still quite bold for a woman—attend medical school. "Isn't studying medicine," she asks Condy, "better than piano-playing, or French courses, or literary classes and Browning circles?" (III, 103).[4]

So far the novel is likely to appeal to all independently minded people. The "conventionality" that Blix protests against is the same "conformity" against which idealistic Americans from Emerson to David Riesman have warned. Certainly, too, the "functions" against which Blix revolts are stultifying enough—a round of dinners, teas, and dances at which the same people continually meet and gossip for fear of being called—as Blix is—*déclassé* if they fail to attend. This rebellion against a deadening round of empty forms is Thoreauvian, and her encouraging Condy to quit "faking" and to go out and write from experience would have warmed the hearts of the transcendentalists.

Unfortunately, the weakness of the novel is that the cure Norris proposes is little less jejune than the disease. Blix and Condy, as she has revamped him, are obviously intended as models; but, although they are superior to the idle society they reject, they are hardly admirable specimens themselves. For example, Blix's character is apparent from the first, adjective-loaded description of her as "good, sweet, natural, healthy-minded, healthy-bodied . . , honest, strong, self-reliant, and good-tempered" (III, 4). Readers may also note that she "dissuaded" her young brother from playing with a neighboring dentist's son who had St. Vitus' dance and that her younger sister is approvingly described as "tractable." Blix behaves contemptuously toward an awkward Irish maid and addresses an unfamiliar Chinese restaurant owner as "John." Her "sincerity" seems to be simply a self-righteous disregard for the feelings of other people.

Blix and Condy are completely self-centered. Other people are simply "projects" to them, as is demonstrated by the way in which, with Norris' amused approval, they "arrange" on the basis of their own condescending stereotypes the romance between two writers to the lovelorn column. They are completely indifferent to others' problems or motives, probably because they are almost stupefyingly naïve about them. As Maxwell Geismar stresses in *Rebels and Ancestors,* Condy and Blix, despite their revolt, remain "extravagant and self-indulgent" members of the leisure class who live in "a narrow and narcissistic little world of social superiority."

Perhaps nothing damns both author and characters more than the way in which Norris, without a trace of irony, describes Condy's enthusiastic response to Blix's suggestion that the simple tale of an ordinary man's poetic experience (as a diver, he decides not to surface a young girl's corpse) be vulgarized by adding a "surprise ending" (years later he goes down for the girl again and doesn't come back up) which displays the complete lack of ability to participate in another human's feelings that John Steinbeck, for example, castigates in "The Leader of the People."

The intellectual poverty of this supposedly admirable pair is emphasized by the way they concentrate—again with the author's obvious blessing—upon "technical points" in their reading. Condy is particularly proud that he and Blix have noticed the accuracy of one small engineering detail in a Kipling story, although neither evidences any interest in what—if anything—the story is about. Condy, who is going to be a writer himself, is interested in accumulating such "points." He is pleased to learn that one *kills* instead of *catches* a fish and that one paints the name of a ship on the *counter* not the *garboard streak.* He picks up his nautical lore from the lighthousekeeper's wife who is reading an encyclopedia straight through. One gathers that Norris admires especially those who might become so incensed over the use of an anachronistic axe in *The Cherry Orchard* that they wouldn't bother to notice why the trees were being cut down.

Another evidence of the immaturity of the novel is Norris' falling back at last upon the hoary device of the *deus ex machina* to resolve the situation. When Blix and Condy decide at last that they are really in love, she will not give up the idea of going to medical school in New York (in order to be "doing something"), although she has admitted that she has no idea of practicing. Nor can Condy think of a way to dissuade her, technical "points" being of little use in such matters. They are saved from living blighted lives when a letter that Condy failed to read because it accompanied a rejected manuscript proves to be an offer of an assistant editorship in the big city. Whether this ending proves that self-proclaimed virtue always triumphs or that the Centennial Publishing Company is attuned to the rhythms of nature is left to the reader. All we can say is that, if the novel is supposed to provide a design for living, the model is risky.

Occasionally in *Blix* Norris touches upon serious matters, but never for long. The young lovers are surprised, for example, to hear the lighthousekeeper they admire speak of participating in adventures that their society would label immoral. The opportunity, however, to probe the question of how to respond to a person one likes as an individual but whose behavior violates one's ethical code is dissipated when the man's wife insists that his talk is all just "yarns" to "show off." Insincerity is all right so long as it is amusing and poses no problems. Blix's objections to conventionality, for that matter, did not arise until a drunkard's request for a dance was made so suddenly that she "hadn't time to think" and "was all confused—mixed up" (III, 18).

The worst thing about *Blix* is that there is no evidence Norris did not intend it to be taken seriously. Light-hearted romances about superficial people can be amusing if the author has the depth the characters lack and remains distant enough from them to evaluate their behavior accurately. When, however, his thinking is as superficial as his characters', the result is a work whose only lasting value is—like *Moran of the Lady Letty's*— as a case study.

From the viewpoint of one who values human dignity, Norris' characters are a vast improvement over the idle scandalmongers they rebel against; but they are far from being what they might. Those who feel rather than think and are prey to phantasms replace malice toward those who differ from them only with contempt and indifference and become involved with things rather than people (hence the number of talented but illiberally educated young people who are attracted into the sciences because there, as one physicist recently stated, they can "escape people").[5]

Norris' weakness was that he mistook naïve and prejudiced individuals who have just begun to become really responsible for themselves, for those truly "decent" human beings who have achieved some sensitivity to the universal problems of man. *Blix* is the measure of his inadequacy—a book that illustrates the important point that even those who can distinguish what is wrong often have only a shadowy notion of what is right.

III *Golden Girl of the West*

A Man's Woman (1900), Norris' third Valkyrie fable (Lloyd Searight differs from her predecessors only in that she has "dull-red" hair) is usually grouped with *Moran* and dismissed as a trivial adventure story. The dismissal is justified, but the classification is erroneous. As Grant Knight perceived, "the internal evidence is that Norris meant it to be a serious commentary upon contemporary relations between the sexes."[6] Probably dissatisfied that the idyllic tale of Blix spelled out with sufficient energy the secret of the benevolent cosmic forces to which man ideally attunes himself, Norris set out to substitute bombast for wheedling. The resulting novel is an even greater disaster than the ill-fated polar expedition it describes because, as Knight further observes, Norris had embarked upon "an undertaking for which he was not equipped."

Norris' notion about the secret of harmonious relations between the sexes is not too obscure. Most of the novel is devoted to establishing the characters of the unbelievable hero and heroine, two of the most thoroughly obnoxious characters ever to be treated sympathetically in fiction. Ward Bennett, the hero, is an intrepid explorer of the icy wastes. His principal characteristics are faulty mentality (he cannot remember whether he has sent an important message and he cannot entertain alternate hypotheses), fantastic strength and endurance, and an absolutely inflexible insistence on commanding other people (he tells a subordinate who reports seeing a light, "You don't see any signal until I choose to have you"). The heroine, Lloyd Searight, registered nurse, is, like Blix, a rich girl who has broken with convention and busied herself managing other people's affairs. She has "no vast love for humanity," but has entered her profession because "to *do* things had become her creed . . . not to think them . . . not to talk them . . . not to read them" (VI, 49).

Ultimately when Ward's best friend is gravely ill with an infectious disease, "these two characters of extraordinary power" engage in a clash of wills which ends with Lloyd's capitulation and her admission that she loves Ward. Norris makes clear that this is the way things should work out when he comments, "They two, high-spirited, strong, determined, had clashed together, the man's force against the woman's strength; and the woman, inherently weaker, had been crushed and humbled." Lloyd's opportunity comes, however, when—rather than conceal the truth that Ward has forced her to give up nursing the friend— she confesses voluntarily and wins "the struggle with self, the greatest struggle of all." Norris moralizes: "Against the abstract principle of evil the woman who had failed in the material conflict with a masculine, masterful will had succeeded, had conquered self, had been true when it was easy to be false, had dared the judgment of her peers so only that she might not deceive" (VI, 204).

The lessons of masculine superiority and utter sincerity taught, Norris is unwilling to call it a day. He introduces a new complication when the two principals, upon deciding to marry, announce also that they will give up their lifeworks—Lloyd, by tearing up a telegram requesting her services on a difficult case; Ward, by tossing away a book about Arctic exploration. Norris hastens to assert, however, that these two gestures are not equally well advised: "Lloyd's discontinuance of her lifework had been in the nature of a heroic subjugation of self. Bennett's abandonment of his career was hardly better than weakness. In the one it had been renunciation; in the other surrender" (VI, 207). The unfortunate result is that "in the end . . . it was the woman who remained the stronger." Before the book could be ended, the balance must be redressed and the man and woman must accept their traditional nineteenth-century roles.

Whatever the reader may think of Norris' theories about sexual inequality, he is likely to be either more amused or outraged than impressed by the way in which the final problem of getting Ward back on the job is solved. After wrestling with cosmic forces for two hundred pages, the author can find no way to teach the lesson he wishes except by conjuring up a flag-waving *deus ex machina*. Lloyd has already asked, "Why shouldn't *our* flag be first at the Pole?" But Ward is reluctant to give up the comforts of home for the rigorous abstinence of Kolyuchin Bay.

Lloyd's big chance to get him out of the house and back into destiny's harness occurs when a trio of San Francisco businessmen appear one day and explain:

"We give out a good deal of money . . . but . . . we can feel only a mild interest in the pictures and statues, and museums and colleges, although we go on buying the one and supporting the other . . . what we would most like to aid financially would be a successful attempt by an American-built ship, manned by American seamen, led by an American commander, to reach the North Pole . . . provided *you*, Mr. Bennett, are in comand (VI, 232-35).[7]

They have failed to stir up the necessary patriotic fervor in Congress, however, and the kitty is twenty thousand dollars short. When they ask how they are to raise it, Lloyd rises and says, "You may draw on me for the amount." Hearing her, Ward at last "understands," and the end of the novel sees him afloat once more and headed "due north."

The novel has all the usual Norris touches—formless fears of self-indulgence, a puritanical repression of feelings, and contempt for "inferior" races (even though an Eskimo has suffered through the horrors of a futile flight across polar ice with a party of explorers, he "could not be trusted with the lives of all of them"). Its failure, however, is not attributable solely to Norris' awkward attempts to work out a theory of man's destiny, for he does this in all of his novels. When he deals in *The Pit* with less superhuman figures, he manages to depict successfully the triumph over selfishness that he fumbles in *A Man's Woman*.

The trouble with this novel is, first, that it differs from *Moran* in that too little happens in it. Norris disobeys his own injunction to let the story speak for itself and spends far too much time in a woolly discussion of vast abstract questions of right and wrong. Even in the dramatic parts of the book, he fails to be interesting because he obviously has no firsthand knowledge of his material. John Sherwood has demonstrated in "Norris and the *Jeannette*" (*Philological Quarterly*, April, 1958) that Norris drew most of his first two chapters from the published accounts of the experiences of the survivors of the destruction of the ship *Jeannette* in the Arctic Ocean in 1881.

Such use of secondhand material was especially disastrous in the work of a writer like Norris, whose most enduring writing records his personal observations. In *Blix*, he even contrasted the two kinds of material a writer may use when he explains that in preparing an article about a ship Condy Rivers "either could fake his copy from a clipping on the subject . . . or he could go down in person to the wharf. . . . The former was the short and easy method. The latter was more troublesome, but would result in a far more interesting article" (III, 22-23). In *A Man's Woman*, Norris fakes. Small wonder that in a letter to Isaac Marcosson he confessed himself discontented with the novel.[8] Another such and he might have become one of those cranks with private theories about human behavior who rifle libraries for obscure erudition to use as a backdrop for stories about characters that bear not the slightest relation to normal human beings. What Norris says of Ward Bennett—"normal vision was denied him"— is true of all the characters in this essay on the role of the sexes.

Fortunately—since novelists of distinction are rare and cranks abound—Norris chose to return to reality with a work that, while it also illustrates his obsession with great themes, has long attracted readers not with its generally overlooked philosophy but its powerful picture of contemporary disaster.

IV *Woman's Place*

Before dismissing the three rather fumbling novels of Norris' "middle period," we should note that they are related by the author's preoccupation with the problem of the proper relationship between the sexes. All three are concerned with forceful women who revolt against the frustrating inhibitions of conventional society. Since Norris is sympathetic with the rebels, his novels at first seem contributions to the movement that was growing rapidly during his lifetime to grant equal rights to women.

Norris, however, would probably have had little sympathy with the Suffragettes. Although he endorses a practical education for women in *Blix* and *A Man's Woman*, he makes it unmistakably clear in all three novels that a woman must give up her career when she marries and that, when grave decisions are to be made, she must submit to the man. In his private life, Norris apparently insisted upon all the prerogatives of the Victorian male. His friend Juliet Wilbor Tompkins writes that he was "unwaveringly master in his own house" and that, when he laid down the law, his wife obeyed.[9] He appears to have felt—like many earlier nineteenth-century tractarians—that the woman's place was definitely in the home and her role was to exercise a tranquilizing and ennobling influence upon her husband.

Indeed there is little evidence that Norris was interested in procuring women's rights as such. Rather he was generally concerned that both men and women should intuitively respond to the rhythm of nature, "think" rather than "feel," as Blix and Lloyd Searight did. He was interested not in advocating a particular reform but generally improving a decadent, "unnatural" society. As documents in the history of the "woman question" his novels offer, therefore, only evidence of the persistence to the dawn of the twentieth century of the traditional attitude that woman's "influence" was properly exercised only in "retired spheres."

CHAPTER *6*

A Large Enough View

THE TRADITIONAL interpretation of *The Octopus* (1901) is summarized in the description of the novel in *The Oxford Companion to American Literature* as "dealing with the raising of wheat in California, and the struggle of the ranchers against the railroads." Coming as it did when the abusive practices of the railroads and the agitation of the enraged farmers were about to lead to major reform legislation, *The Octopus* has often been identified as either a result of the powerful Populist movement of the 1890's or a foreshadowing of the muckraking books of the early twentieth century—a kind of companion piece of Upton Sinclair's *The Jungle.*[1]

Although Norris in 1899 wrote to a Mrs. Parks that he was firmly "enlisted upon the other side" from the railroad trust and did not consider the Southern Pacific "legitimate or tolerable,"[2] there is no evidence that he was actively interested in the Populist movement. The only specific political reference in the novel is a derogatory mention of Lyman Derrick as the candidate of the "regular Republican" party (II, 358), and in both *The Octopus* and *A Man's Woman,* Norris offers encomia to enterprising, dynamic San Francisco businessmen. There is little evidence of any very liberal political leanings on the part of a writer who allows a sympathetically presented manufacturer to say of himself and an editor, "I don't think his editorial columns are for sale, and he doesn't believe there are blow-holes in my steel plates . . . also it appears that we have more money than Henry George believes to be right" (*A Man's Woman,* VI, 231). Ernest Marchand wondered why Norris had suddenly become interested in sociological questions when he came to write *The Octopus,* for "not a whisper" of such occurrences as the Homestead and Pullman strikes are heard in his earlier books. The answer very probably is that Norris was not so much interested in specific problems as in finding illustrations for his general theories of the proper conduct of life. We shall see that he does not really sympathize with either side in the struggle he depicts in *The Octopus*. He appears to have embraced Populist causes only when these chanced to coincide with his preconceived notions; and, although Norris was associated with *McClure's*, one of the magazines most closely connected with the muckraking movement, he left its employ and New York without regret before the movement had gotten up full steam.

As early as the socially conscious 1930's, in fact, reformminded critics began to doubt if *The Octopus* was even the work of the socially enlightened determinist that Norris was sometimes reputed to be. Granville Hicks pointed out in *The Great Tradition* that it was impossible to reconcile a strict determinism with a faith in all things working inevitably toward the good, and others were quick to seize his point and to charge Norris with being "confused." That critics might have been confused and Norris perfectly consistent but misunderstood seems not to have occurred to anyone until the vogue for social reform literature had begun to wane with the passing of the worst of the Depression.

The road to a greater understanding of Norris' "lost frontier" epic was paved in 1940 by "Norris Explains *The Octopus*," an article in which H. Willard Reninger compares the novelist's critical theories with his practice. Citing the shepherd Vanamee's important conversation with the poet Presley near the end of the novel, Reninger points out that the whole work demonstrates the viewpoint Vanamee enunciates when he tells his listener that if he looks at disaster "from the vast height of humanity . . . you will find, if your view be large enough, that it is *not* evil, but good, that in the end remains" (II, 345). Thus Reninger explains that the "alleged inconsistencies" in the novel are reconciled by an all-encompassing philosophy:

> The novel dramatizes the doctrine that although men in a given locality can be temporarily defeated by combined economic and political forces, which in themselves are temporary and contigent on a phase of civilization, the *natural forces*, epitomized by the wheat, which are eternal and resistless, will eventually bring about the greatest good for the greatest number.[3]

Reninger's analysis is helpful, but not sufficiently critical of Norris' failure to carry out his theories. Reninger cites the novelist's demand that artists probe deeply into the motives of those "type men" who stand for the multitude, but he does not observe that Norris understood little about underlying human motives and that he usually brushes aside hard-to-analyze behavior as instinctive. Reninger takes Norris' ideas too much at their author's declared value; and since he dismisses Vanamee's mysticism as "merely a technique" Norris used, he fails not only to ask why only the shepherd is triumphant in his quest but also whether Norris was really conscious of all the ideas that influenced his interpretation of the events he employed.

Weaknesses of previous interpretations of the novel, including Reninger's, are well demonstrated in George Meyer's "New Interpretation" (*College English,* March, 1943). Meyer is the first to point out that Norris' opinion of the ranchers in the novel has been misconstrued and that he saw them not as "poor folks" —like the migrants in *The Grapes of Wrath* or victims of the system like the workers in *The Jungle*—but as "reckless would-be profiteers, as speculators so unfortunate as to be less powerful and ingenious than their competitors in a ruinous struggle for economic power."

He also corrects a long-standing misapprehension of the book by identifying Shelgrim, the railroad president who talks of nature in order "to rationalize his own irresponsibility," and not Norris as the fatalist. He also points out that the poet Presley is not a self-portrait of the author and that the tragedy depicted here need not invariably be repeated, because the reader can learn from the misfortunes of others. He recognizes, too, that the novel is a kind of transcendentalist tract illustrating Norris' "conviction that Americans wrought unnecessary evil by supporting an economic system that clashed violently with the facts of nature," the principal one of which is that "the wheat will flow irresistibly from the field where it is grown to mouths that need to be fed" and that the natural force of the movement "injures or destroys many individuals unlucky enough to be standing in its path."

Meyer's article might have provided a definitive reading of the novel if he had not considerably overestimated the author's capacity for abstract thinking. When he insists that Norris thought that, if men would cooperate with one another, they might eliminate the disastrous role that chance plays in human affairs, he fails to see the significance of the Vanamee subplot (he treats the shepherd only as a mouthpiece for certain views), and he ignores Norris' frequently reiterated preference for *doing* over *thinking*, since cooperation with other men (although not with the "forces of nature") requires even more thought than action.

A careful, thorough, rational scholar himself, writing during a period of grave international crisis, Meyer fails to give sufficient emphasis to the mystical elements in Norris' thought, his pre-occupation with "sixth senses," and his disdain for liberal educa-tion. The critic tries too hard to make the novel fit the pattern of the traditional reformist tract because he does not see that Norris was as suspicious of cooperation between individual men as he was of conflict between them.

Both Reninger and Meyer are correct in perceiving that *The Octopus* is internally consistent, but neither pays sufficient atten-tion to the extent to which irrational elements influenced Norris' thought. Only by careful examination of the Vanamee subplot is it possible to observe the extent to which Norris tried to in-corporate a good example, as well as several horrible ones, into the first volume of his epic trilogy.

This subplot has not always received the attention it deserves, because in *The Octopus*—as in other works—Norris' skill as a reporter caused the depiction of specific evils that were not his essential concern to overshadow the general moral he wished to convey. Although the book has been often reprinted and sum-marized, we should perhaps before beginning an analysis recall the major events of the involved plot Norris built around the notorious Mussel Slough affair, in which the exploitative practices of the railroads led to armed rebellion.[4]

It is not always sufficiently acknowledged that the novel is an exercise in point of view. What it contains is what Presley, a poet somewhat reminiscent of Edwin Markham, sees during a summer that he spends in the San Joaquin Valley trying to dis-cover a purpose and a direction for his own work. He is a guest of Magnus Derrick, an ex-governor who farms one of the largest ranches in the valley. Unfortunately Derrick—like most of his neighbors—does not have clear title to his property. Much of it belongs to the Pacific and Southwestern Railroad, "The Octopus," which has promised—but not contracted—sometime to sell the land to the ranchers at a low price. A crisis is precipitated when, at the height of a party, news arrives that the railroad demands that the ranchers either pay an exorbitant price for the properties they have improved or be evicted. When the railroad attempts to have a Federal posse evict the ranchers, an armed battle ensues in which six of the ranchers—including Derrick's son and his neighbor, Annixter—are killed. Derrick is further discredited when it is revealed that he has used bribery to buy a position on the state railroad commission for his son Lyman, who sells out to the railroads anyway. Like Curtis Jadwin in *The Pit*, Magnus Derrick speculates desperately and is utterly shattered.

Others suffer as well. Dyke, a loyal employee whom the railroad unjustly discharges and then bankrupts, turns train robber and goes to prison. Mrs. Hooven, widow of one of the ranchhands killed in the skirmish, starves to death in San Francisco. Even Behrman, the principal agent of the railroad, who seems immune to human justice, is—in one of Norris' most spectacular scenes—finally smothered in the hold of a ship that is being loaded with his own wheat. Presley survives, but he leaves California, saddened by the death of his friends and convinced that he is ineffectual as either poet or man of action.

The only major character to survive the holocaust is Vanamee, a shepherd who some years before the story begins had withdrawn from society after his sweetheart was mysteriously assaulted and died in childbirth. Living close to nature, he has developed mysterious telepathic powers, and he is finally rewarded for his renunciation of self-destructive ambition by winning the love of his former sweetheart's daughter.

All of these events are usually interpreted as adding up to an attack upon the railroad and to a paean of praise for the wheat—the irresistible life-force that frustrates those seemingly beyond the reach of human justice. Such an interpretation does not, however, satisfactorily explain all of the novel—especially the concluding sentiment that "in every crisis of the world's life . . . if your view be large enough . . . it is *not* evil, but good, that in the end remains."

A good approach to the matters needing attention is through Donald Pizer's recent "Another Look at *The Octopus*," which restates Meyer's interpretation of Norris' attitude toward the ranchers as "speculators" and adds two further observations that aid understanding of the novel. First, Pizer shows that the story essentially concerns educating the poet Presley into a recognition of the insignificance of the individual in comparison to the operation of the great, benevolent forces of nature. Then he points out the novel's relationship to transcendental thought.

Basically, Pizer maintains, Norris is looking not confidently forward but nostalgically backward, since his "faith in individual perception of Truth and in the concomitant dependence upon a benevolent nature in discerning this Truth found its most distinctive statement in the transcendental movement."[5] Pizer argues, as I do throughout this study, that Norris—driven by fear and distrust of contemporary civilization—sought principally to turn back the clock.

Ironically, Norris might have produced a more impressive work if he had been less nostalgic. As an angry plea for the rectification of specific evils, *The Octopus* is one of the most powerful tracts ever penned. Those who extract the story of the struggle between the ranchers and the railroad from the rest of the book are to a certain extent justified by the result. Judged, however, on the basis of what the author, and not posthumous editors, considered essential, the work fails to convey its full message convincingly not because of internal inconsistencies— since the final pages advance arguments that reconcile seeming internal contradictions—but because of the lack of examples to support these arguments adequately. In the long run evil may be less enduring than good, but Norris as a journalist depicts the short-range victory of evil more convincingly than as a novelist he demonstrates the ultimate triumph of good.

But about the supposed inconsistencies—charges that the novel is confused have generally centered upon two passages: Presley's incredible interview with Shelgrim, a railroad president apparently modeled on Collis Huntington of the Southern Pacific, and the concluding statement that "all things, surely, inevitably, resistlessly work together for the good."

Certainly the Shelgrim episode (II, 281-86) distorts the structure of the novel and begins to make us suspect the artistic integrity of a writer who peremptorily introduces a new viewpoint into a nearly completed work. To claim, however, as Ernest Marchand does, that after the interview "Norris walked arm in arm with [Presley] and shared his bewilderment" is to continue the unjustified identification of author and his character and to miss the real point of the incident.

During the interview, Shelgrim makes the often quoted statement, "You are dealing with forces, young man, when you speak of Wheat and the Railroads, not with men. . . . If you want to fasten the blame of the affair at Los Muertos on any one person, you will make a mistake. Blame conditions, not men" (II, 285). Presley regains the street "stupefied." He cannot refute this new idea, which "rang with the clear reverberation of truth" and he asks if anyone were "to blame for the horror at the irrigating ditch" where so many of his friends died.

These doubts, however, are Presley's, not Norris'. What has happened here—as elsewhere—is that Norris has botched the writing. The book is easily misread not because it expresses subtle ideas—the thinking is often quite simple-minded—but because Norris' writing about ideas is often muddy, and it is not easy to distinguish between what he thinks and what his characters think. We must recall, however, that despite the furore over his poem "The Toilers," (a work similar to Edwin Markham's "The Man with the Hoe"), Presley—as shown by an unsuccessful speech he delivers to a group of ranchers and by his abortive bombing of the villain's house—is not effective as either thinker or doer, as a handler of either symbols or things.

Far from identifying himself with Presley (although they share some ideas), Norris throughout the book treats the poet with mild contempt as a "type" illustrative of the ineffectiveness of the literary man in coping with the violent forces in the world.

That Norris was also not taken in by the arguments he assigns Shelgrim is demonstrated later when at a society dinner he depicts Presley beginning to think things over and—in what Maxwell Geismar calls "the intellectual climax of the novel"— realizing that he has been duped by the fast-talking Shelgrim:

> The railroad might indeed be a force only, which no man could control and for which no man was responsible, but his friends had been killed, but years of extortion and oppression had wrung money from all of the San Joaquin, money that had made possible this very scene in which he found himself. . . . It was a half-ludicrous, half-horrible "dog eat dog," an unspeakable cannibalism (II, 317).

Presley foresees that some day the people will rise and in turn "rend those who now preyed upon them." As George Meyer points out, Shelgrim uses "natural forces" as a rationalization for his own irresponsibility. Despite his high position, the railroad president is simply a confidence man, one who overwhelms counter-argument by a skillful use of question-begging and of faulty dilemmas (irresponsible operation or bankruptcy.)

Norris puts his finger on the real trouble when he says that "No standards of measure in [Presley's] mental equipment would apply to [Shelgrim] . . . not because these standards were different in kind, but that they were lamentably deficient in size" (II, 284). The forces at work are not necessarily uncontrollable (Marchand points out that "the growing of wheat is not a cosmic process, but a purely human activity"), but they cannot be controlled by the characters Norris has created.

To dwell on the insufficiency of his characters' mental equipment, however, would defeat the author's purpose, for it would conflict with the uncritical enthusiasm he expresses elsewhere when he asks about his "sturdy American" actors: "Where else in the world round were such strong, honest men, such strong, beautiful women?" (II, 217). The question is intended to be rhetorical; but it might be answered, "Anywhere that people are strong-minded enough to control the forces civilization has created." Norris has not proved that these forces cannot be controlled, but only that he cannot conceive the characters who could control them. He then proceeds to display unfounded confidence in himself by assuming that he knows as much about human capability as anyone.

This unwarranted confidence is responsible for what many readers consider the dogmatism of the conclusion. How did Norris know that "all things surely, inevitably, resistlessly work together for the good"? Why, he just knew it, and the reader who will not take his word for it is obviously as much out of harmony with the secret forces of nature as the ill-fated ranchers of the San Joaquin Valley. Part of the strength of Norris' work is that he never felt any doubt about his own perspicacity.

Probably more as model or "type" than proof of his theories, Norris did weave into his epic tale of the fall of the foolish, the tale of Vanamee as a kind of counter-narrative to guide those who seek the right road. This story is not usually credited with its proper importance in the over-all design of the novel, for the lonely shepherd is often ignored or mentioned only as spokesman for the philosophy that colors the final pages of the book. Yet even if Norris had not especially spoken in a letter to Isaac Marcosson of this subplot as "even mysticism . . . a sort of allegory,"[6] the amount of space he lavished upon the story and the fact that it is Vanamee's philosophy that is repeated at the end of the book should alert readers to the significance of the only major character in the story who emerges triumphant.

The shepherd enunciates the philosophy that "in every crisis of the world's life . . . if your view be large enough . . . it is *not* evil, but good, that in the end remains." We need not, however, take his word for this; his own story is supposed to illustrate the truth of the premise just as much as the story of the ranchers and their struggle against the railroad is supposed to illustrate the truth of the premise that those who stand in the way of irresistible forces will be destroyed.

Vanamee is a kind of latter-day Thoreau, "a college graduate and a man of wide reading and great intelligence, [who] had chosen to lead his own life, which was that of a recluse" (I, 33). Unlike Thoreau, however, his withdrawal from society is not an experiment, but a permanent policy. In view of the final contrast between what happens to him and to the others in the novel, we must conclude that Norris thought that the sensitive, introspective person could regain harmony with nature only by completely rejecting civilized society.

Vanamee loved Angèle Varian, who lived on a flower ranch near the mission where he met her nightly. One night, however, Angèle was met by a never identified "other," who raped her. When she died in childbirth, "the thread of Vanamee's life had been snapped" (I, 37).

As a result of his long isolation from society, Vanamee has developed a strange power to call other people to him. ("If I had wanted to, sir, I could have made you come to me from back there in the Quien Sabe ranch," he tells a priest.) He does not understand this power himself ("I understand as little of these things as you," he tells the priest, when asked about the power [I, 133]). Finally after eighteen years he returns to the scene of Angèle's rape and begins calling for her, demanding that God answer with "something real, even if the reality were fancied" (I, 145). Through a succession of scenes, we see the answer to this totally irrational call gradually materialize until at last "Angèle was realized in the Wheat" (II, 347).

The "answer" is Angèle's daughter, who has come in response to Vanamee's mysterious calls and who even more mysteriously loves him as her mother did. Her coming demonstrates specifically how good—in the large enough view—comes out of evil. The rape and death of Angèle were evil, but the child born of this bestiality is good. Norris even has Vanamee make this point specifically: "I believed Angèle dead. I wept over her grave; mourned for her as dead in corruption. She has come back to me, more beautiful than ever" (II, 345).

Does this example prove the sweeping generalization Norris makes at the end of the book? Probably many critics have overlooked the whole business because few could concede that it did. Even if we were willing to grant that one example might be enough to support a theory about the operation of the Universe, we could not overlook the extraordinary aspects of the particular situation—Vanamee's mysterious ability to use a kind of telepathic hypnosis (he speaks of a "sixth sense" or "a whole system of other unnamed senses" experienced by "people who live alone and close to nature"), and Angèle's daughter's remarkable duplication of not only her mother's appearance, but also her feelings.

What is Norris trying to say here? We cannot, of course, disprove telepathy, "sixth senses," and the transmigration of souls that he seems to be hinting at any more than he can prove their existence with this wild romance that most critics of the book have apparently found too embarrassing to discuss. But what we can say is that it is hard to imagine what Norris does mean if not that we must either put up with injustice and abuse, temporary "evils" of civilization, or else reject civilization altogether and take to the woods where we can develop "unnamed senses." If man's problem is to improve conditions in the world he has made, Norris is no help. He is rather like the man who, unable to do something himself, announces that it cannot be done and sits scoffing at those who try. Although he lived in a society full of worshippers of progress, with whom he is sometimes confused, he himself is a self-appointed propagandist for "hard" primitivism.

Another indication of the backwardness of Norris' thought

is the really most remarkable part of the interview with Shel-grim, the railroad president—not the blatant sophistries about "forces," but the vignette of Shelgrim granting another chance to a drunken bookkeeper, an act that shatters Presley's concept of the executive as a bloodsucker. The reader may well ask along with Presley how the man who can handle an erring underling so intelligently and humanely can have treated so in-humanely the ranchers and Dyke, a once faithful employee whom the agents of the "octopus" drive to robbery, murder, and death.

The answer is that Shelgrim, as Norris conceives of him, is not really a competent administrator of a vast business, even though Norris may have drawn the incident from his own know-ledge of the railroad executives. Actually the behavior that it illustrates can best be analyzed in the light of a passage from Steinbeck's *The Grapes of Wrath,* in which a dispossessed tenant ponders:

> "Funny thing, how it is. If a man owns a little property, that property is him, it's part of him, and it's like him. . . . Even if he isn't successful, he's big with his property. . . . But let a man get property that he doesn't see, or can't take time to get his fingers in, or can't be there to walk on it—why, then the property is the man. He can't do what he wants, he can't think what he wants. The property is the man, stronger than he is. And he is small, not big. Only his possessions are big—and he's the servant of his property."[7]

This is a classic statement of the view of the "thing-handler" as opposed to the "symbol-handler"—that man can understand only that which he can actually see and feel. The tenant has grounds for his observation, because many men who have actually only the education and intelligence to be "thing-hand-lers" have been forced into or have taken upon themselves the roles of "symbol-handlers," with the distressing result that conditions occur like those depicted in both *The Octopus* and *The Grapes of Wrath.*

Actually Norris foreshadows part of Steinbeck's tenant's speech in his analysis of Magnus Derrick, the elder statesman among the ranchers:

> It was the true California spirit that found expression through him, the spirit of the West, unwilling to occupy itself with details, unwilling to wait, to be patient, to achieve by legitimate

plodding. . . . It was in this frame of mind that Magnus and the multitude of other ranchers of whom he was a type, farmed their ranches. *They had no love for their land.* They were not attached to their soil. . . . To get all there was out of the land, to squeeze it dry, to exhaust it, seemed their policy. When, at last, the land worn out, would refuse to yield, they would invest their money in something else; by then, they would all have made their fortunes. They did not care. "After us the deluge" (II, 14; italics mine).

The charge here is the same as that against the bankers in *The Grapes of Wrath*, and those who have supposed that Norris was as critical of the ranchers as of the railroads have been right as far as they have gone; but they should have gone further. He is actually more critical of the ranchers, because the point of the incident of Shelgrim's kindness is to suggest that he does actually love those around him—those with whose problems he is personally acquainted.

What Norris failed to see is that a man of such limited vision would be incompetent to operate successfully a vast railroad or any comparable enterprise since he would be unable to do what competent administrators of vast affairs must do if they are not to court disaster—set up and administer equitably and impartially uniform regulations for those with whom they deal directly and those with whom they do not. Of course such competent administrators were uncommon in the nineteenth century (they are still not especially abundant), but commercial disasters were fairly common. Many businesses and institutions (including the railroads) are still paying for the incompetence of the "self-made" administrators of the Gilded Age. Norris' shortcoming was that he reported ably enough what he saw, but he failed to perceive what was wrong. He stepped into the trap that awaits many uncritical admirers of the empire builder— the assumption that those who have the force and energy to put together an empire necessarily have the intelligence and patience to administer it adequately. A reporter, of course, would not be handicapped by making such an erroneous assumption, but it is likely to prove crippling to a man seeking to formulate rules for the conduct of life.

Ernest Marchand is right when he says that the real struggle in *The Octopus* is between "two types of economy"—the old, vanishing agricultural, and the rising industrial; but he does not see that both economies are administered in this novel by the same type of chieftain, since the author had no concept that a more complicated economy demands a new, more thoughtful type of leadership.

Norris got close enough to the ranchers to see their weaknesses, but he did not get as close to the managers of the railroad. *The Octopus* has often been called one-sided, but it has not been pointed out that the result of the oversimplified treatment of the railroad's role in the controversy is that it actually comes off better than it might because Norris was too busy looking for evil to notice incompetence. Shelgrim easily rationalizes away charges of malfeasance by blaming evils on forces rather than men, but he could not so easily dispose of charges of misfeasance or non-feasance.

Norris' naïveté in the presence of empire builders recalls that the one striking exception to his attack upon civilization is his praise in *A Man's Woman* and "The Frontier Gone at Last" of those conquerors of the physical frontier who are now tackling the economic frontier. In "The True Reward of the Novelist," he had also observed that the "financier and poet" are alike, "so only they be big enough" (VII, 17). He was probably dazzled enough by Huntington, who supported the *Wave,* to suppose him a truly great and good financier, just as he probably supposed himself a great and good artist.

An illustration of his susceptibility to the word-magic of the business titan occurs in *The Octopus* when Cedarquist, a prominent industrialist, after denouncing San Francisco's failure to support *his* iron works, which he calls an "indifference to *public* affairs" (my italics and shades of Charlie Wilson!), goes on:

> "The great word of the nineteenth century has been Production. The great word of the twentieth century will be—listen to me, you youngsters—Markets. As a market for our Production . . . our *Wheat,* Europe is played out. . . . We supply more than Europe can eat, and down go the prices. The remedy is *not* in the curtailing of our wheat areas, but in this, we must have new markets, greater markets. . . . We must march with the course of empire, not against it. I mean, we must look to China (II, 21-22).

What Cedarquist advocates is not spreading civilization, but simply disseminating stuff—things not ideas. He simply seeks to exert some mysterious power over others, and he is no more willing than Vanamee to accept responsibility for it. His talk of "marching with the course of empire" simply advocates doing rather than thinking—action for its own sake, like the irresistible action of unthinking nature.

From this passage we can see how Norris can speak of nature at times as indifferent and yet at others as good. By· *indifferent,* he does not mean what a non-teleological thinker would. He probably could not even conceive of the universe without "a sense of obligation" that Stephen Crane personifies in a poem. *Indifferent* to him simply means *unconscious.* Nature, he feels, does good without thinking about it—but it does do good in the long run. Indeed his opinion is that most of the trouble begins when people start thinking instead of feeling. Without thought, of course, one can have no sense of responsibility; but this did not disturb Norris, for he assumed that one who acted according to the proper "natural" feelings could do no wrong and would not need to worry about consequences.

We should not be surprised, however, that Norris does not insist that his characters be responsible for their actions, since he is irresponsible himself. His lack of responsibility, in fact, accounts for some of the most striking features of *The Octopus.* An example is a section of the novel which some critics have praised in which glimpses of Mrs. Hooven starving to death outside are alternated with glimpses of the guests of a railroad magnate gorging themselves on fancy food inside (II, 302-22). Actually this is one of the most meretricious pieces of writing in the novel since it directly contradicts Norris' principle of writing about representative situations in order to lead to general statements about the operation of the universe. Here he uses a most extraordinary coincidence to agitate the reader's feelings. The point is not that readers should not be moved by Mrs. Hooven's sufferings and infuriated that they can occur in such a place, but that—if Norris' main point that everything works inevitably for the good is true—the sensations provoked by this incident are gratuitous. Such material has a place in the novel of social protest, but here Norris appears merely to be exploiting misery in order to display his talent. He is obliging the reader to indulge in the worst kind of sentimentality—to revel in feeling for its own sake, a kind of emotional masturbation. It is not surprising that the man capable of producing this passage completely

failed to understand Harriet Beecher Stowe's motives in writing
Uncle Tom's Cabin.

Another big scene—that in which S. Behrman, the agent of the
railroad whose principle is "all that the traffic will bear," suf-
focates in the hold of a wheat ship—is suspect for different
reasons. Coming near the end of the novel, the scene at first
appears a masterpiece of ironic symbolism: Behrman, seemingly
impervious to any attack by man, is overwhelmed at last by the
irresistible force of the wheat he had hoped to exploit. The fat,
rich man is killed by the very substance that promises life to
starving Asiatics. The scene very well demonstrates Norris'
doctrine that men, "motes in the sunshine," might perish while
the WHEAT remains (II, 360; capitals Norris').

Yet once again in creating this scene, Norris was gambling—
quite successfully—that the reader would respond uncritically,
unthinkingly. Behrman had been depicted in such a way that
the reader would wish to see him punished for his offenses and
would view the suffocation as a punishment—the wheat operating
not as an indifferent force, but as a *deus ex machina.* To see what
is wrong with the scene we need to remember that the incident
could have happened to anyone; there is nothing earlier in the
novel nor in the scene itself that justifies interpreting Behrman's
death as retribution, except our own feelings.

As Charles Walcutt points out in *American Literary Naturalism,* Behrman is an unsatisfactory character anyway, since "his
actions could be explained only by a deep-seated hatred which he
is not shown to harbor." In medieval literature, he would be a
stock figure—Mephistopheles, a manifestation of complete evil,
immune to human attack; but in "naturalistic" fiction, he is incredible unless the work is intended primarily as a morality play.

Perhaps, however, Norris was being truly naturalistic and
emphasizing the irony of the coincidence that Berhman, in-
vulnerable to other men, was killed during a moment of triumph
by natural forces beyond his control. Why then have the wheat—
which in this book has been endowed with a special symbolic
significance as a *creative* force—do the dirty work? It would be
far more naturalistically ironic to have this self-controlled,
scheming man inconspicuously killed in a situation he had no
part in creating—by a bullet intended for another or a falling
object. Actually Norris is trying to provide further evidence

that things work inevitably, irresistibly for the good by having benevolent natural forces dispose of Behrman, but he forces his point. Sending the forces of nature to do a man's specific job both overly sentimentalizes nature and excuses man's irresponsibility—including the artist's when he falls back on gothic machinery to dispose of behavioral problems he has raised.

Earlier in this chapter, I questioned Norris' artistic integrity. The scenes I have just discussed are further evidence that defending this book against its earlier critics does not vindicate it but simply brings to light more serious flaws. But lest it appear that my only aim is to "debunk" *The Octopus,* I must make it clear that the novel is a magnificent imaginative achievement, one of the few American novels to bring a significant episode from our history to life in such a way that the reader feels he is participating in the ponderous events. Like *McTeague, The Octopus* compensates for its defects with vivid reporting. When we strip away the naïve arguments and the blatant attempts to titillate the reader's sentiment, we uncover a remarkable panorama of the life of a confused society torn between its desires, on the one hand, to return to the irresponsible, formless life of the frontier and, on the other, to move on to a state that might be more stable but also more chafing because one's rights and responsibilities would be spelled out by regulations.

Norris was consciously trying to produce an epic. He called his work "The epic of the Wheat," and he twice insists on comparisons with Homer (I, 42; II, 216). Despite his avowed lack of interest in style, he experimented with epic devices in this novel. The long scene in Annixter's barn was obviously influenced by the description of revels in the Homeric poems, and it even pretends to poetry through the use of refrains ("Two quarts 'n' a half. Two quarts 'n' a half." "Garnett of the Ruby Rancho, Keast from the ranch of the same name"), and they are justified only as they tie together the whirl of scenes composing this long, climactic chapter.

In a great measure, Norris himself wrote the work that he demands in "A Neglected Epic," the tale of the conquest of the West that would "devolve upon some great national event" and depict a hero who "died in defense of an ideal, an epic hero, a legendary figure, formidable, sad," who "died facing down injustice, dishonesty, and crime; died 'in his boots'" (VII, 49). Annixter meets the requirements—the clumsy misogynist who learns to love first his own wife, then "others," until his love expands to embrace the whole world on the very day that he rides to his death in defense of his homestead.

Curiously, most epics appear not at the zenith of the societies they celebrate, but in their dying days. Milton definitively stated a theology that was just losing its grip on the minds and hearts of men; Dante gave final form to the neat pigeonholes of medieval cosmology just as this rigidly structured era was about to collapse into the Renaissance; and that even Homer wrote during the last days of the patriarchal society he depicts is suggested by the mildly satirical treatment of those gods who must earlier have been fervently worshipped. By the time a way of life has become clearly enough defined and seriously enough threatened to need defending, it has usually lost its impetus and is about to collapse from physical, intellectual or moral defects.

The Octopus is the epic of the conquest of the frontier by powerful, undisciplined forces. *Doing* rather than *thinking* was needed to overcome vast and often hostile geographical forces. But with the frontier gone, the kind of freedom it had permitted and even demanded for its conquest could only either disappear too, or turn upon itself self-destructively as it does in the battle between the rancher and the railroad here celebrated. Not long after the publication of *The Octopus,* both sides were to find that because they had failed to discipline themselves they were subjected to increasing external regulation, and "frontier psychology" was to become an anachronism after the last claims were staked. Some have speculated that *The Octopus* helped to bring about the regulation of the conditions it describes, but it is more likely that the regulation was already imminent, since, like many epics, the novel dealt with conditions that could not have persisted much longer.

Like *McTeague, The Octopus* is a valuable document because it expresses a philosophy that is not a lesson to its time, but a reflection of it. Norris could not achieve the detachment of a Conrad or even a Crane, because his own ideas, fears, and prejudices were too much like those of his characters. His lack of artistic integrity is not the result of hypocrisy, but of inadequate self-analysis. In his behalf it must be pleaded that he was not like the artistic prostitutes of Madison Avenue and Hollywood who cynically manipulate the public for their own temporary advantage. Rather he was like his own characters—

especially Shelgrim and Magnus Derrick, the leaders of the contending parties, who were giants in their own time—whose offense was not that they deliberately did wrong but that because of adolescent self-infatuation, they failed to perceive the limitations of their own powerful gifts.

Norris did not really know how to cope with the evils of his times; he could only advise flight. Yet he enables us to see why his contemporaries could not cope with these evils. *The Octopus* is quite unintentionally a powerful tract, because the author who trusted action over thought shows us the dangers of sharing his beliefs.

CHAPTER 7

"It's When You Are Quiet
That You Are at Your Best"

THE PIT (1903), Norris' last novel and second volume in
the never-completed wheat trilogy, has had a curious history. Until recently, it was by far his most popular work. The
original trade edition sold more than twice as many copies as
those of all of his previous novels combined, and *The Pit* was
the first of his works to be made into a successful play and
motion picture. Most critics, however, beginning with Dreiser
who called it "a bastard bit of romance of the best seller variety,"
have regarded the novel as a distinct disappointment after *The
Octopus.* Such a judgment may, however, only reveal the immaturity of the critic's taste, for the novel is more carefully
thought out than its predecessor and is, in fact, the only work
in which Norris shows promise of achieving intellectual maturity.

One advantage the author had in writing this novel is that in
it—for the only time except in the lightweight *Blix*—he dealt
with the kind of people among whom he had grown up and
whom he knew best. At last he moves to the center of his stage
the people like Cedarquist, whom he handled authoritatively
but had relegated to a minor position in *The Octopus.* He also
had the advantage of having severely disciplined himself while
preparing to write this novel.

Mathematics had always been Norris' weak point, so that
financial operations had been a mystery to him. Progressive
educators would say—probably correctly—that he had never been
adequately motivated to tackle the difficult, abstract subject.
If he was to write convincingly of the operations of the wheat
market, however, he had to understand something about them.
Franklin Walker reports that George Moulson spent many even-
ings inducting Norris into the secrets of speculative finance

with clever "teaching devices." The instruction paid off. If Norris had been equally assiduous in learning something about the construction of long fiction, *The Pit* might be one of the most effective American novels. Because of the author's disdain for "style," however, the work is awkwardly patched together in a manner that obscures its "message." Even in this ungainly pile—something like the Jadwin mansion that plays a large role in it—we can, however, trace the outlines of the story Norris had so long been trying to tell of the struggles of the *nouveau riche* to understand themselves.

The novel is usually treated as the dramatic story of Curtis Jadwin's effort to corner the Chicago wheat market, based on the famous attempt in 1897 by Joseph Leiter. Actually, however, the story of the corner provides only background for understanding the critical episode in the education of Laura Dearborn Jadwin.

Laura is another girl like Blix and Lloyd Searight (*A Man's Woman*), for she, too, rebels against the petty restraints of a hidebound society. Born in a small Massachusetts town where the "New England spirit" prevails, this spirit appears to her "a veritable cult, a sort of religion, wherein the Old Maid was the priestess, the Spinster the officiating devotee, the thing worshipped the Great Unbeautiful, and the ritual unremitting, unrelenting Housework" (IX, 40).

When the neighbors begin to interfere actively in Laura's life, she flees to Chicago, where she finds three suitors. When one of them is too bold, she rejects them all; but Curtis Jadwin, a financier, will not be refused. Dazzled by the promise of the opulent life his wealth will make possible, Laura marries him; but the life of "conspicuous consumption" proves insufficient to hold the couple together. Bored, Jadwin—who had renounced speculation—begins to plot a corner of the wheat market. As he becomes more and more engrossed in his scheme, he drifts further and further from his wife. Laura, affronted, feels that he no longer thinks her beautiful and plans to run off with a doting artist, Sheldon Corthell. Jadwin's corner almost succeeds; but, encouraged by the rising prices the corner has produced, farmers plant heavily. Unusually favorable growing conditions result in a bumper crop that Jadwin cannot corner; again the Wheat has triumphed over man's selfish machinations. Ruined, Jadwin returns home on the night that Laura has agreed to run away with her lover; but she—seeing at last where her duty lies—chooses instead to go West with her husband to help him build a new life.

Ernest Marchand echoes the views of many critics, beginning with William Dean Howells, when he says that Laura's marital problems are "overprominent" in the novel. Charles Walcutt in *American Literary Naturalism* even goes so far as to say that "obviously, she is . . . merely a foil to set off the great struggles in the Pit." Yet although the Pit scenes are the most exciting in the book, far more of the story is devoted to Laura's problems; it would be odd for a novelist to devote most of his book to a side issue. In "Norris and the Responsibility of the Novelist" (*South Atlantic Quarterly*, October, 1955.) Charles G. Hoffmann soundly surmises that the love story is the central matter in the novel, but that its importance has been obscured by the expectation of a social message raised by *The Octopus* and by the stylistic effectiveness of the Wheat Pit scenes. He also wisely compares the book to *The Rise of Silas Lapham*, for which Norris has Curtis Jadwin express admiration. Hoffmann does not, however, treat in detail the evolution of Laura's attitude, and only by following her story closely can we see why the book reaches the conclusion it does.

Laura's troubles begin when her adventurous spirit is cramped by the decadent busybodies in her home town in New England. Her neighbors are suspicious of her because she belongs to the Episcopal rather than the Presbyterian church and employs servants, but the "crisis" comes when she travels alone to Boston to hear Modjeska in *Macbeth* and upon her return broaches the idea of acting herself:

> A group of lady-deaconesses, headed by the Presbyterian minister, called upon her, with some intention of reasoning and labouring with her.
>
> They got no farther than the statement of the cause of this visit. The spirit and temper of the South, that she had from her mother, flamed up in Laura at last, and the members of the "committee," before they were well aware, came to themselves in the street outside the front gate . . . all confounded and stunned by the violence of an outbreak of long-repressed emotion and long-restrained anger, that like an actual physical force had swept them out of the house (IX, 40-41).

Within a month, Laura leaves her home town for Chicago.

What Norris succeeds in doing in this novel that he had not before is to show the tremendous expense of spirit necessary to carry out such a rebellion. The stubborn pride that makes the gesture possible lingers on after the revolt has succeeded, in the form of excessive love of self and suspicion of others. Having struggled desperately to achieve individuality, Laura finds it difficult to assume a satisfactory role in society. She could easily have become a fanatic like Olive Chancellor in James's *The Bostonians.*

She shies away from marriage because she fears that, in the "pitiless" man's world of the turn of the century, she will lose through marriage the individuality that she has purchased at the price of exile from her home. Having escaped one oppressor—bigoted New England society—she is not anxious to submit to another. Yet, paradoxically, she is attracted to forceful men; in them she sees kindred spirits. Although Corthell, who designs stained-glass windows, would do her bidding, she cannot bring herself to love him: "The figure that held her imagination and her sympathy was not the artist, soft of hand and of speech, elaborating graces of sound, and colour and form, refined, sensitive, and tempermental; but the fighter, unknown and un-knowable to woman as he was; hard, rigorous . . . conspicuous, formidable . . ." (IX, 60).

When one of her suitors kisses her without permission, she feels that her suspicion that men will exploit her is confirmed, and she decides to break with all who are courting her rather than tolerate indignities. Corthell, who takes her at her word, goes off to Europe; but Jadwin refuses to be put off. Spurned, he pursues her more assiduously than before. At last he wins her.

Laura is still not willing, however, to admit that she loves him. She is depressed that "love" is not so exciting and flattering to her vanity as she had hoped; she still thinks of love as based primarily on physical attractiveness. She has already had doubts about Jadwin because, although she prefers the fighter to the artist, she prefers the sensuous self-indulgence of the studio to the Sunday School that Jadwin teaches. In learning to look out for herself, Laura has lost interest in looking out for others.

Although an older married woman tells her that the kind of "love" she is looking for is "what you read about in trashy novels" (IX, 153), the young woman says that she is marrying Jadwin

for what he can give her: "Think of it, the beautiful house, and
servants, and carriages, and paintings, and, oh honey, how I will
dress the part." Warned that she should not marry for "things,"
she scoffs, "I would marry a ragamuffin if he gave me all these
things—gave them to me because he loved me" (IX, 161-62). In
return she vaingloriously supposes that she is desirable because
her "grand manner" becomes a wealthy hostess, who should
be "respected," despite the fact that in actuality her manner
"never helped her popularity" (IX, 164, 338).

She still thinks of love as a one-way street. When her sister
asks if Laura loves Jadwin, she is told: " 'Indeed not. I love
nobody. . . . I wouldn't give any man that much satisfaction.
I think that is the way it ought to be. A man ought to love a
woman more than she loves him. It ought to be enough for him
if she lets him give her everything she wants in the world . . .
it's her part, if she likes, to be cold and distant. That's my idea
of love' " (IX, 159). She marries and, despite her fantastic ego-
tism, things proceed smoothly for three years. The couple's
energies are consumed in getting accustomed to living on the
grand scale in the mansion Jadwin builds on fashionable North
Avenue. That they are basically still small-town people is illustrated by Laura's aunt's bewildered speech when she sees the
house: " '. . . it's all very fine, but, dear me, Laura, I hope you
do pay for everything on the nail, don't run up any bills. I don't
know what your dear father would say. . . . Thirty-three [electric
lights, which she supposes "new-fangled" gas devices] in this one
room alone. . . . I'd like to see your husband's face when he
gets his gas bill' " (IX, 206).

Affluence, like independence, proves a strain upon a girl
reared in a traditional, frugal community:

> For very long [Laura] found it difficult, even with all her
> resolution, with all her pleasure in her new-gained wealth, to
> adapt herself to a manner of living upon so vast a scale. She
> found herself continually planning the marketing for the next
> day, forgetting that this was now part of the housekeeper's duties.
> . . . She was afraid of the elevator and never really learned how
> to use the neat little system of telephones that connected the
> various parts of the house with the servants' quarters. For months
> her chiefest concern in her wonderful surroundings took the
> form of a dread of burglars (IX, 200-1).

There is something pathetic about these people with "too much, too soon" who are overwhelmed by wealth they had not been trained to enjoy. Norris' persistent fears of getting too far away from nature were probably largely inspired by the hothouse atmosphere in which he had been reared. Eventually, however, the Jadwins become acclimated to "conspicuous consumption." When they do, he gets bored with showing off the house and yearns for more excitement ("I just about know [the neighboring] park by heart . . . how would you like to go to Florida?" he asks Laura.) She succeeds in fitting herself into her new surroundings by exercising "a curious penchant toward melodrama," which enables her to act the part of "a great lady" with "all the superb condescension of her 'grand manner' " (IX, 202). She begins to think of herself as "two Laura Jadwins"— "one calm and even and steady," who "adored her husband, who delighted in Mr. Howells's novels, who adjured society and the formal conventions, who went to church every Sunday" and "the Laura of the 'grand manner,' who played the role of the great lady from room to room of her vast house . . . who was conscious and proud of her pale, stately beauty" (IX, 239-40).

Although Jadwin had promised to stop speculating, boredom drives him to begin again:

> "What are we fellows, who have made our money, to do? I've got to be busy. I can't sit down and twiddle my thumbs. And I don't believe in lounging around clubs, or playing with race horses, or murdering game birds, or running some poor helpless fox to death. Speculating seems to be about the only game, or the only business that's left open to me—that appears to be legitimate. . . . It's fine fun" (IX, 221).

His rapid rise to success has not been accompanied by a corresponding intellectual development. Nor could Laura be the expected help to him because, as Corthell points out when she indicates her fondness for a painting by Norris' old master Bouguereau, her tastes are shallow. She likes it, she says, "because it demands less" than others, "pleases you because it satisfies you so easily" (IX, 235-36).

A later sentimental novelist would have straightened matters out by hinting the approaching patter of tiny feet. Norris even intimates at one place (IX, 190) that matters might have been improved if the Jadwins had started a family; but, as William

Dillingham points out, Norris is still too much in the genteel tradition to discuss sexual problems openly.[1] Although Norris mentions rape in *The Octopus*, he is as reluctant as Howells to refer to the normal sexual intercourse of a married couple.

The breach between the couple widens. As Jadwin becomes more and more obsessed with his effort to corner the wheat market, Laura takes up various fads and even entertains Corthell in her private rooms. She makes a desperate effort to win back her husband's devotion on her own terms, for the idea of considering another's feelings is still as alien to her as to most of Norris' characters. Supposing that lack of beauty and glamour is her defect, she lures Jadwin to spend one evening at home and entertains him not as "a calm wife" but as "a grand lady."

In one of the most effective evocations in any fiction of the garish taste of the *nouveau riche*, Laura first appears before her husband costumed as the Emperor Justinian's consort Theodora and recites a passionate scene from Racine's *Athalie*. Then as Bizet's Carmen, "a red rose in her black hair, castanets upon her fingers," she dances a passionate Bolero. Jadwin simply finds what can only be described as his wife's attempt to seduce him "sort of overwrought" and protests, "I like you best when you are your old self, quiet, and calm, and dignified. It's when you are quiet that you are at your best" (IX, 298). Still the country boy at heart, he has too much respect for this elegant woman he has won to realize that she may be more than another public showpiece.

But even the old, calm, quiet self fails to hold Jadwin when his broker calls; although her husband maunders about the good, old, simple life back on the farm, neither of the two Laura Jadwins can distract him from the pit. Still convinced that American women lose their hold over their husbands because they cease to fascinate them with superficial beauty, Laura tries to win back Jadwin with an ultimatum that if he loves her, he must spend her birthday, June 13, with her. But this is the day that Jadwin's attempt to corner the wheat reaches its climax.

Despite her high-handed tactics, Laura has had, even before the critical June day, a vague intimation of approaching disaster and has decided that "if anything happened to Curtis, her place was at his side" (IX, 337). Her resolution is, however, still not firm; and, when Jadwin fails to come home as promised one night, she is tempted to send for Corthell.

On her birthday Laura begins to see the light. Her sister Page, who has been an uncomprehending observer at the wheat pit that morning when Jadwin's corner collapsed, tells Laura that she has failed her husband because she does not care enough about his business: "'Just think he may be fighting the battle of his life down there in La Salle Street, and you don't know anything about it—no, nor want to know. "What do you care about wheat," that's what you said. Well, I don't care either, just for the wheat itself, but it's [her fiance's] business, his work; and right or wrong . . . good or bad, I'd put my two hands into the fire to help him'" (IX, 383). At first Laura is simply angry, thinking "even if he had been very busy, this was her birthday. . . . She had known the humiliation of a woman neglected. But it was to end now; her pride would never again be lowered, her love never again be ignored" (IX, 385-86). Afterwards, however, she begins to have misgivings:

> Was it—after all—Love, that she cherished and strove for—love or self-love? . . . Was this, after all, the right way to win her husband to her—this display of her beauty, this parade of dress, this exploitation of self? . . . Had she been selfish from the very first? . . . Dimly Laura Jadwin began to see and to understand a whole new conception of her little world. . . . She had been accustomed to tell herself that there were two Lauras. Now suddenly, behold, she seemed to recognize a third—a third that rose above and forgot the other two, that in some beautiful, mysterious way was identity ignoring self (IX, 387-88).

Although the language is overblown, Norris is attempting to describe Laura as a person who has risen above selfish considerations and learned to love another well enough to put the other's interests before her own. The transformation of Laura's personality, however, is not unbelievably abrupt. Despite her dawning realization of what selfless love is, she still wishes to hold her husband to her demand that he spend this night with her. He fails to appear, and Corthell arrives instead. In a last fit of self-pity, Laura pleads that the artist make her love him and forget all that has happened. They agree to run away together the next night.

No sooner has Corthell gone, however, than Jadwin appears "his eyes sunken deep in his head, his face dead white, his hand shaking." As they sit close together, "groping in the darkness," she hears the newsboys crying, "Extra . . . all about the Failure of Curtis Jadwin!" (IX, 394-95). Instead of running off with Corthell, Laura sells her property and goes west to start a new life with her husband, who tells her that "we both have been living according to a wrong notion of things" (IX, 400).

Jadwin's false notion is more apparent and has often been discussed. His attempted corner succeeds as long as his manipulations do not boost the price above what wheat is actually worth; but his troubles begin when he reckons without the forces of nature and, driven by the same kind of self-love that makes Laura wretched, begins to scoff at expert reports of a bumper crop and to feel that he can drive wheat to the abnormally high price of two dollars a bushel.

He rationalizes his folly by telling his wife, "I corner the wheat! Great heavens, it is the wheat that has cornered me. The corner made itself. I happened to stand between two sets of circumstances, and they made me do what I've done" (IX, 270). Obviously, though, he is using this deterministic argument (as Norris himself was likely to use talk of "forces") to avoid accepting the responsibility for his personal vanity and "wrong notions." Although it is the sheer volume of wheat flowing into the market that breaks Jadwin's corner, he would never have gotten into trouble if he had stayed home in bed.

Although *The Pit* contains one passage, which—like the end of *The Octopus*—talks about the wheat "obeying" laws of supply and demand (IX, 358), Norris, by the time he wrote his last novel, was ceasing to rely upon the notion that man was a passive agent helpless in the hands of the vast impersonal forces of nature. He offers, through the broker Gretry, the explanation —much more convicing than Jadwin's—that the speculator "put wheat so high, that all the farmers planted it, and are getting ready to dump it on us" (IX, 353). How Jadwin has literally been driven mad by his infatuation with speculation is evident from his physical attack on the faithful but cautious Gretry for "selling out."

The title of *The Pit* is not often enough recognized as having a double meaning. Besides referring to the room where wheat trades are consummated and around which much of the action of the novel whirls, it refers also to the abyss that Norris has spoken of as early as *Vandover*—the pit toward which people are hurled as the indulgence of their self-love causes them to attempt to thwart what the novelist calls "the resistless forces of nature." Both Jadwins head for this pit; the husband topples over; but, as more convincing evidence of Norris' theory that good comes out of evil than he had been able to provide in *The Octopus*, the wife hears the news of the husband's disaster just in time to prevent her from following his course to a disastrous end. Ernest Marchand is unfair when he calls the end of the novel "anti-climatic, too trivial"; it is the climax that Norris has been building up to from the beginning—the wheat corner entered halfway through the action—and is trivial only if domestic relations are less consequential than business deals.

Norris accomplishes his purpose in *The Pit* without recourse to the mystical trappings and remarkable coincidences of *The Octopus*. There is an occasional mention of a "sixth sense," but generally Norris uses the term in this novel only as a metaphor to describe Jadwin's knack for correctly evaluating situations until his lust for power blinds him.

Because the characters and events are convincingly human— drawn from observation rather than myth—*The Pit* is the only one of Norris' novels that can be read enjoyably today except as a period piece. Although it preserves a splendid picture of the *nouveau riche* of the period (excellently illustrating what Veblen meant by "conspicuous consumption"), the preservation of a vanished mode of life is not the principal justification for reading it today.

Norris in most of his novels approaches his ideas about universal principles of good behavior through specific problems that have either diminished in significance (*The Octopus, A Man's Woman*), or that he was not equipped to understand (*Vandover, McTeague*). In *The Pit*, however, he deals with people he knows well (there are remarkable superficial resemblances between his parents and the Jadwins) and with problems that are still urgent. Ernest Marchand points out that the Jadwin story is essentially an anti-gambling tract. Although the regulations of the Securities and Exchange Commission have largely eliminated utterly irresponsible speculation, the gambling instinct and the overconfidence bred of temporary success are related problems that are not only still with us in everything from personal to international relations, but that probably always will be with us.

The increasing flow of fictional and factual writing about

marital dissatisfaction and the discord resulting from self-love and self-indulgence also shows that these problems are constantly looming larger or are more frequently recognized than before. While writing his last novel, Norris seems to have realized at last that appealing as the desire to return to a kind of unconscious, uncivilized life might be, it was wishful thinking. Only at the end of his short life does this man who is often classified as a naturalist seem to have absorbed the basic premise of scientific thought—that any program for reform must begin with a dispassionate acceptance, not an emotional rejection, of things as they are found. Jadwin's unsound intuitions about the wheat suggest that Norris may even have begun to distrust "feelings."

We wonder if Norris may have been conscious of the extent to which Laura Jadwin's problems paralleled his own. Like her, he had been torn at the beginning of his career between a concept of art as something detached from life (which led to his absorption in the Middle Ages) and the magnetic attraction of the street (which accounts for his fascination with the Mc-Teagues). Like her, he decided in favor of the street; but still he was repelled at the same time he was fascinated.

His attempts to court the favor of the "street" led only to a pulp adventure like *Moran*, and Norris may have recorded, through the story of Overbeck's seduction by the "literary women" in his short story "Dying Fires," an experience like Laura's temptation to give up Jadwin and run away with Corthell. Certainly the small success of Norris' efforts to write for the "street" and to share his views about the proper relationship between man and woman must have distressed him as much as Laura's failure to reclaim Jadwin from the Wheat Pit.

Whatever unidentified spark ignited his desire to write the Epic of the Wheat led him back, however, to his concept of the novelist's responsibility. Possibly his shocked reaction to the dreadful sights he had seen while a war correspondent in Cuba awakened him to the need to try to get back on the "right track," the "natural course." Possibly his marrying and becoming a father awoke a sense of mature responsibility.

Whatever happened, *The Pit* seems more genuinely the result of intensive self-analysis than any of Norris' earlier novels. Although this last novel is less immediately gripping than *Mc-*

Teague or *The Octopus,* it is a more notable achievement because Norris, while writing it, appears for the first time to have been really conscious of the precise implications of his story. It is also to *The Pit's* credit that it has been the most often misunderstood of Norris' novels, since the more searchingly a book probes the motivations underlying human behavior, the less likely it is to yield its secrets to superficial readers. Like Laura Jadwin, Norris —despite his penchant for melodrama—was at his best in his quiet moments when he promised to become an author who would explore rather than merely denounce the problems of urbanized society.

CHAPTER 8

Stubble

BESIDES THE exotic experiments of his college days and his seven novels—a staggering body of work for a single decade by any standard—Norris managed to write a sizable group of miscellaneous short stories, many of which have been undeservedly rescued from the obscurity of the periodicals in which they first appeared. Although it cannot be determined just when these stories were written, they emerged in two widely separated groups, each with distinctive characteristics. The first written between 1895 and 1897, was composed of contributions to the *Wave* and other western papers; the second, of pieces in eastern magazines, principally *Everybody's* between 1901 and 1903. Most bear evidence of having been thrown together so hastily that it is unlikely they were written long before publication—or even before the deadline for the issue in which they appeared. Hardly one adds anything to Norris' stature; indeed he would be as forgotten as Edwin Milton Royle if his reputation depended upon them. A few, however, help round out the knowledge of those underlying ideas that can be derived from his more substantial fiction.

The *Wave* stories (many of which are preserved in *The Third Circle* and *Frank Norris of the Wave*) are of three remarkably dissimilar kinds: fragments from novels, almost incredibly snobbish and sadistic "adventure" stories, and absurdly sentimental sketches. In these, Norris appears to have had an even more conspicuously split personality than the characters from Vandover to Laura Jadwin that fascinated him. Some of these stories, like "Fantaisie Printaniere" and "Judy's Service of Gold Plate" have attracted attention for first mentioning characters in *McTeague*; but Ernest Marchand may be right when he insists that they were simply drawn from materials for the unpublished novel, although they suggest that Norris originally intended to make the book less grim and even less sophisticated than he finally did. An assuredly direct borrowing is the pointless "The End of the Act," which reappears word for word as the beginning of the fourteenth chapter of *Vandover and the Brute*. Slightly revised, "The End of the Beginning" was also to serve as the opening chapter of *A Man's Woman*.

The stories which appear designed to provide sadistic pleasure are among the most astonishing of Norris' works because they seem so entirely out of keeping with the character of a man with any pretensions as a serious artist. Some of them are simply naïve, adolescent outpourings of patriotic sentiments like those the author gave free rein in *A Man's Woman*. In "A Defense of the Flag," an all-American "thoroughbred" (this favorite term of Norris' turns up often in his short stories) quite justifiably removes the green flag with which a group of Irish "clowns" have replaced the American flag on the San Francisco City Hall. Drama degenerates into farce, however, when this son of the original settlers wraps himself in the affronted flag to face the howling mob.

There is less patriotism and more racial prejudice in "The Third Circle," one of Norris' ill-advised imitations of Kipling and his contribution to the drive to warn Americans against the "yellow peril" that led to the Oriental Exclusion Act. In this agitated tract, a white girl who drops in for a cup of tea in a Chinese restaurant and then allows herself to be tattooed, disappears. She is recognized years later as the debauched slave of a Chinese in a subterranean opium den.

"The degenerate Spanish," a favorite target of Norris', are lashed in "A Case for Lombroso," the tale of the way in which a Castilian Miss Hromada, whose "morbid and unnatural" sensitivity makes her "almost hysterical," and whose first cousin must have been Poe's Roderick Usher ("the odour of certain flowers giddied her," "She could feel the spots on a playing card with her finger tips," etc.), turns another "thoroughbred" into a "brute." He takes "a morbid, unnatural, and evil" pleasure in physically torturing and humiliating her, as McTeague does Trina.

Not all evil is attributable, however, to non-Anglo-Saxon blood. In "His Single Blessedness," the indubitably American Doychert, who thought he had to live up to an adolescent remark that he

hated children, so unseats his wife's mind by telling her that he
hates their three-week old daughter that she can never look at
him again or even read his writing without becoming hysterical.

The most inexplicably cruel tale of the lot, however, is "The
Dis-Associated Charities," in which two young men (presumably
"thoroughbreds") having "nothing better to do one evening" go
with a charity worker to a restaurant where blind beggars eat.
They trick three of these unfortunates into running up a bill that
they cannot pay and then pummeling each other until the police
haul them off. All this is supposed to be a grand joke on the
charity worker to whom the incident is never explained, but it
leads the reader to wonder just what kind of mind could invent—
let alone enjoy—such childish humor at the expense of the
handicapped.

All this leering cruelty may have been the result of strong
feelings of depression, for during this period Norris also wrote
"The Puppets and the Puppy," a cheerless "dialogue," in which
a debate about free will between a quarrelsome group of toys is
ended when a puppy breaks into the playroom and destroys all
of them. Arnold Goldsmith makes much of this as representative
of a purely deterministic middle phase in Norris' thought,[1] but
such a short, choppy work in an uncommon vein seems more
like the kind of thing an unstable person would write during a
passing fit of melancholy than a considered statement of a
philosophical position.

Norris' instability is indicated by his vacillating wildly from
pseudo-humorous sadism to sickly sentimentality during this
period when he was trying to cut out a career for himself. "Little
Dramas of the Curbstone" presents us with three children and
their mothers—one child a blind idiot, another a paralytic, and the
third an unidentified type of delinquent who would rather be
arrested than taken home. Norris ties together this seemingly un-
related trio with a speculation concerning the whereabouts of
their fathers and the remark that "the chief actors in these Little
Dramas of the Curbstone had been somehow left out of the
programme" (IV, 25).

One more sample is enough. In "His Dead Mother's Portrait,"
an innocent maker of trout flies who worships the memory of his
supposedly dead mother is held back, by looking at her picture,
from entering "the most disreputable dive in town," where an
old woman dressed as a girl of fifteen does a song-and-dance

act. The magic of the picture evidently keeps him from going insane, like Mrs. Doychert and some other Norris characters, as he might have had he discovered that this debased entertainer is in fact the revered mother. Norris thought highly enough of this plot to write a variation upon it with the mother changed to the title character of "His Sister."

Of the group the only one worth attention, except as a specimen of Norris' work, is "'Boom.'" This story is interesting not because of its awkwardly contrived plot (the rescue of another man driven mad by a misjudgment), but because of its incidentally preserving a well-delineated picture of the aftermath of the real estate subdivision "Booms" of the gaudy 1890's when people squandered fortunes on "developments" marked only by ". . . a lamppost with a tarantula's nest where the lamp should have been" which was "hard to miss . . . as the desert was very flat thereabouts, and the lampposts could be seen for a radius of ten miles" (IV, 53).

All that actually unifies these dissimilar tales is the sentiment we have observed in all of Norris' early fiction—an almost hysterical hatred of a decadent civilization that fosters subterranean opium dens and subdivision "booms." Norris appears to have been one of those people—like his character Blix—who have no patience whatsoever with any kind of imperfection and who are so upset by any evidence of physical or mental degeneration that they can respond only by a sentimental outburst or a violent attack that masks their feelings of great distress. In stories like "The Third Circle" and "His Single Blessedness" a single misstep ruins a person's whole life. Far from being an objective naturalist, Norris was an extremely unrealistic idealist who could not stomach the constant compromise of ideals demanded by life in an urban society.

❖   ❖   ❖   ❖   ❖

Norris apparently abandoned the short story for a few years after his move to New York. During this period he turned out novels in such rapid succession that little time was left for other work. Near the end of his life, however, he returned to the shorter form—probably to supplement his income while involved in the lengthy working out of the Wheat trilogy. Most of the "New York" stories are collected in *A Deal in Wheat and Other*

Stories (1903), although a few appear at the end of *The Third Circle* (1909) and some of the poorest were collected only for the edition of 1928.

The principal distinction between these stories and the earlier ones is their greater morality. Sadism and sentiment are still present, but they are better controlled and the stories have endings that are virtuous as well as dramatically effective. As *The Pit* also illustrates, Norris was veering in a new direction at the end of his career; the praise Curtis Jadwin pays such novels as Howells' *The Rise of Silas Lapham* could well have voiced Norris' own thoughts. As Norris matured, he evidently began to feel that one might not be utterly destroyed by a single misfortune, but might learn from it.

Representative of the grotesque humor of Norris' "final period" is a series of tales which finds fun in the embarrassments suffered by "Three Black Crows" (an American, an Englishman, and a "colonial"), most of whose activities are illegal. The plot of "The Dual Personality of Slick Dick Nickerson," for example, involves the Crows' stealing valuable sea otter skins from a Russian post. Their schemes, however, never work out; in the otter story they are falsely alarmed that the authorities are coming aboard their ship, and destroy the valuable furs. In "Two Hearts that Beat as One," two of the Crows discover that the woman for whose hand they have fought is actually a male Mexican bandit in disguise. A few such adventures should certainly make anyone wish to go straight.

The sentimental tales of the period are less patently moral. Several of them express disturbing fears about an author's losing his creative powers that could easily have been Norris' own. "A Lost Story" tells of a woman who, on the strength of her first none-too-successful volume of short stories, has been hired—as Norris was—as the reader for a prominent publishing house. She has outlined a novel and has been encouraged to write it by one of the outstanding authors of the period—as Norris was encouraged by Howells. Among the manuscripts she is assigned to read, she finds one by an unknown young westerner that tells essentially the same story as her projected work. Torn between the desires to reward a kindred spirit and to eliminate a competitor, she finally rejects the manuscript; but her letter of rejection is returned with a notation that the young man has died. She then proceeds to write her own novel, only to learn from the older writer that the book is a failure, because "the whole animus that should have put the life into it is gone."

What may be signs of even greater personal uneasiness over the kind of loss of "animus" that had first troubled Norris when he was writing *Vandover and the Brute*, provides the substance of "Dying Fires." Overbeck, a young westerner, has had his first book, *The Vision of Bunt McBride*, published, and it is unexpectedly successful. (Norris, it should be noted, used the name "Bunt McBride" himself for a character in some short stories of this period.) The young author is brought to New York and falls into the hands of the "New Bohemians," who advise him to abandon his crude western characters and write about refined city dwellers. When he does, his novel *Renunciations* is called "foolishness" by his publishers, and he is dropped by the "New Bohemians" in favor of a new celebrity. When he returns West (as Norris did himself shortly before his death) to recapture his original inspiration, he finds "the ashes were cold by now."

This melancholy tale of artistic castration fears may have been intended as either a warning to young writers or a slap at some New Yorkers Norris disliked, but it may also suggest his own mood upon abandoning the big city to return to California. Contradictory currents flowed through the work of Norris' last two years, and we cannot even make an informed guess about what might have happened to him if he had lived through the artistically barren first decade of the twentieth century. On the strength of *The Pit* alone, however, he had little reason to feel the fears he voices in his short tales about writers. Although he may not have realized what was happening, his work was beginning to gain in depth of understanding as it became less sensational.

Two short works of this last period are of interest because of their relationship to larger works. "A Deal in Wheat" has been commented upon as often as any of Norris' short stories because of its obvious relationship to *The Pit*. Actually the similarities are superficial. Although both works deal with a wheat corner, the short story is a kind of transitional study that may help explain a shift in Norris' viewpoint between the times he wrote the two volumes of his proposed trilogy. *The Octopus* ended with the generalization that all things work irresistibly toward the good, but "A Deal in Wheat" is obviously the work of a man who is not so sure. The main point of the story is that one who sees both ends of a transaction involved in a wheat corner learns that the farmers and workingmen are ruined, while the great operators remain unassailable. There is no mention of "cosmic forces" in this story; the destructive force is clearly human irresponsibility. Although some of the trappings of cosmic optimism are present in *The Pit,* they are decorative rather than organic to the work, a principal point of which is that something can be reclaimed from disaster only if human beings have learned to abandon their "wrong notions." Jadwin is allowed to rationalize, but only to keep his mind from going, too, once his fortune is gone.

Somewhere in the course of collecting the information about the financial operations he describes in his last novel, Norris had gained a new sophistication. "A Deal in Wheat" seems even less a short story than the writer's way of getting down on paper the observations that had led to a major change in his thinking. If Norris had ever been able to be as coldly analytical in a novel as he is in this one short story, he might have produced a work of intellectual distinction.

Certainly by the end of his life Norris had become capable of a calculating coldness in business that was at least ethically ambiguous, as is illustrated by the remarkable relationship of one of his last works to one of his earliest. The March, 1901, issue of *Everybody's* carries a "new" illustrated story by Frank Norris, "The Riding of Felipe," the kind of tale of old Spanish days in California that readers might have expected from Gertrude Atherton. Upon examination, the story proves not to be "new" at all, but simply *Yvernelle,* the pseudo-epic poem of medieval France that was Norris' first published book, retold in prose against a different backdrop. The works are more than merely similar. "The Riding of Felipe" repeats the story of the poem incident-by-incident from the curse of the temptress to the rescue of the heroine just as she is about to become a nun. Although the short story was collected in *A Deal in Wheat,* there is no comment in the collected edition about the curious duplication.

While it may not be unequivocally unethical for an author to revamp an old work, we certainly suspect his good intentions if he does so silently and presents the new piece as "original." We shall probably never know what prompted Norris to resuscitate *Yvernelle,* although his shifting the setting from medieval

France to nineteenth-century California is in keeping with the Americanization of his post-college work. Perhaps he was rushed to fulfill a commitment; perhaps he wished a return from material that had not paid for itself (Marchand observes that he never wasted material); perhaps, like Overbeck in "Dying Fires," he was trying to recapture his original inspiration; perhaps he was merely curious to see whether the work would succeed better in a new costume. If his motive was the latter, he was doomed to disappointment.

Read together, however, "The Riding of Felipe" and "Dying Fires" do suggest that during the period between the writing of the two novels about the Wheat—probably when he was exhausted from the effort called forth by *The Octopus*—Norris had had doubts about his artistic future and had begun to scrape the barrel. These doubts could have prompted his determination to learn "new things" which led him through writing *The Pit* to a greater success after his death than he had known during his too brief life.

CHAPTER *9*

Cricket Chorus

G ULLEY JIMSON, free-lancing hero of Joyce Cary's *The Horse's Mouth,* speaks of critics disdainfully but not inappropriately as "crickets." The shade of Frank Norris might listen to the cricket chorus with mixed emotions since it has treated him in general with kindness but not especially with discernment. Discussions of his work suggest that even among those who should labor to establish artistic standards, the appetite for flashy melodrama has been insatiable. Except for the unsmiling rear guard of the ebbing genteel tradition, the American idea among critics—as among bankers, and builders, performers and patrons—has been that irresponsibility should be rewarded if only it is spectacular enough.

Since the self-denominated genteel monopolized organs of opinion during the 1890's, early reviews of Norris' lurid tales were generally chilly.[1] Only William Dean Howells, the great champion of youthful talent, gave the disturbing San Franciscan support. *The Pit* was more enthusiastically received than earlier works; but, as Ernest Marchand points out, for three decades after Norris died little was written about him except lamentations over his premature demise and reminiscences of friends and acquaintances like Isaac Marcosson, Hamlin Garland, and Channing Pollock.

Only two essays from this long period are worth preserving. By far the more influential was Howells' long memorial tribute in the *North American Review* of December, 1902, which not only set the tone, but also actually provided the great bulk of judgments for three decades of writing about Norris. Howells' emphasis upon Norris' reliance on Zola has proved the stumbling block of subsequent criticism. He also inhibited later critics by not only limiting Norris' writing worthy of posterity's attention to *McTeague* and *The Octopus,* but even by specifying what would become the standard approach to these works: "Both are epical, though the one is pivoted on the common ambition of a coarse human animal, destined to prevail in a half-quackish tragedy, and the other revolves about one of the largest interests in modern civilization." We should recall also that Howells was himself an imaginative artist when we are confronted with his debatable analogy of *McTeague* and *The Octopus* as "The *Iliad* to its *Odyssey*" in crystallizing contemporary sentiments about the "continentality" of the young novelist's works.

The only comprehensive survey of the whole body of his work by an original reviewer of Norris' books, after the excitement stimulated by his furious production and unexpected death had died down, is in Frederic Taber Cooper's *Some American Story Tellers*. One of the first to challenge the pigeonholing of Norris among the naturalists, Cooper said: "It is impossible to read Norris' works without perceiving from first to last there was within him an instinct continually at war with his chosen realistic methods; an unconquerable and exasperating vein of romanticism. . . ." But the implications of this statement were not explored for several decades. Since Cooper was aware of the importance of Norris' critical essays to an understanding of his fiction, of the "strong underlying note of primevalism" in him, and of the immaturity that made *The Octopus* more impressive as a whole than as a collection of parts, his essay provides a remarkable assessment of the author's achievements and weaknesses that was not to be superseded for twenty years.

Only as an example of the critical prejudices of the smug decade before World War I and of the unbalanced assessments of Norris is there any lingering interest in an essay in John C. Underwood's *Literature and Insurgency* (1914), in which Henry James is attacked at length for becoming an expatriate and a collection of plot summaries is concluded with the observation that "Frank Norris deserves to be ranked slightly higher in the human scale than Mark Twain; and it is quite possible that in the long run his work will be remembered longer."

Literary historians did not agree. Surveys written before 1932 generally granted Norris only a few paragraphs or pages in which he was grouped—following Howells's lead—with Stephen Crane as a specimen of blighted promise. Vernon Parrington might have remedied matters, but the fragmentary notes he left about Norris provide no new insights. The novelist fared better at the hands of the "interpretive biographers" of the 1920's who could weave garlands of words around a few wisps of fact. Charles Caldwell Dobie's "Frank Norris, or Up from Culture," first published in the *American Mercury* in April, 1928, and then used as an introduction to Volume VII of the Collected Works, is far more useful as an example of the kind of romance presented as fact so loved during the "boom" than as a study of Norris.

Dobie's essay, however, survives as part of the first great contribution to the serious study of Norris, the ten-volume collected edition of his works. Before 1928, study of the author was handicapped because much of his work was out of print, and some of it uncollected from the obscure periodicals in which it had first appeared. The attractive, readable, uniform edition of his works facilitated their critical consideration.

Unfortunately, this edition, although it includes a whole volume of previously uncollected works, leaves much to be desired. For some reason, the volumes were not numbered to indicate either the order of the composition or the publication of the works. Many periodical contributions—admittedly of slight value—were not reprinted. The introductions are uncritical —some of them nostalgic reminiscences of Norris' family and close friends; some of them (like Dobie's) simply fulsome attempts to stir up the reader's interest. There is no attempt to provide detailed histories or serious analyses of the books. Biographical data is scattered among the introductions, and there is neither index nor bibliography. Something of the scholarly qualities of those responsible for the edition is indicated by their breaking up the manuscript of *McTeague* in order to include a page in each set of the limited Argonaut Edition, which was simply the regular edition lavishly bound.

Although regrettably a commerical rather than a scholarly venture, the collected edition of Norris, with its bold golden sheaf of wheat on a black binding and its large, uncrowded pages is still one of the most striking sets of books to preserve the major works of an American author. The contribution of this edition to stirring up the study of Norris became apparent in 1932, the single year to produce the greatest spate of writing about him.

The most important addition to the small shelf of books about Norris in that year was Franklin Walker's exhaustive, carefully documented biography. Although hardly critical of his subject, Walker provided an account of Norris' early life and a chronology of his writing that made inexcusable thereafter errors like that of supposing *McTeague* to have been written after *Moran*, which had plagued early studies of the novelist. Little really significant information about Norris has come to light since the appearance of Walker's book; and until some does, there is little occasion for another purely factual account of the author's rather uncomplicated life.

Walker was not the only writer to accord new attention to Norris in 1932. In four literary histories published that year and one the next—by Joseph Warren Beach, V. F. Calverton, Granville Hicks, Grant Knight, and Ludwig Lewisohn, respectively—the finality of Howells' opinions was at last challenged. Enough time had passed and readers' sensitivities had undergone enough shocks so that Norris no longer appeared the radical innovator he had once been. Both Beach and Knight stressed the conventionality of some of his work. Beach found Norris more reminiscent of Edith Wharton than of Dreiser and said that "the quaint familiarity" of *The Pit* gave a sense of "a willingness to accept conventional patterns in human motivation and behavior." Knight, in *American Literature and Culture,* brought out the similarity of *Moran* to the despised "pulp" adventure stories and described the "example to younger men" offered by Norris' fantastic industriousness as more important than the books themselves.

Calverton and Hicks went further in upsetting previous assumptions. In *The Liberation of American Literature,* Calverton identified Norris as one of the originators of the "defeatist mood" in American literature; in *The Great Tradition,* Hicks stirred up the long controversy over the "inconsistencies" in Norris' thought with the observation that the author vacillated between free will and determinism in *The Octopus.* Possibly most unexpected of all was Lewisohn's statement in *Expression in America* that of Norris' work only *McTeague,* written from some obscure inner need, was worth preserving. The rest he called rhetoric.

The groundwork seemed laid for a stimulating critical controversy that might have led to a sweeping reassessment of Norris and his works; but the national Depression inhibited the production of critical books. The only other important work about Norris to appear during the 1930's was the scarce mimeographed biographical and bibliographical guide prepared under the general editorship of Joseph Gaer as the third monograph in the California Literary Research Project sponsored by the WPA (Works Progress Administration).

Activity picked up slowly in the 1940's. The essays by Reninger (1940) and Meyer (1943), already discussed in connection with *The Octopus,* marked the first attempts to apply the close-reading techniques fostered by the New Criticism to Norris. Between the publication of these essays, Norris received an impressive amount of attention. Charles Walcutt began with a brief note in 1941, the writings that were to culminate fifteen years later in *American Literary Naturalism.* Oscar Cargill (*Intellectual America*), Alfred Kazin (*On Native Grounds*), and Walter Fuller Taylor (*The Economic Novel in America*) studied Norris' relationship to significant trends in American intellectual history, and Ernest Marchand provided in *Frank Norris, A Study* (Stanford, 1942) the first full-length analysis of the major influences upon the novelist's thought that at last accorded Kipling, Stevenson, Richard Harding Davis, and Jack London the places they deserve beside Zola.

Although Marchand concluded with a tribute to Norris' artistic skill, the novelist did not fare well in this important group of books. Critics were now far enough away from him to be aware of his deficiencies, but still too close to be patient with them. Cargill took him to task for using a "popular superstition" about uncontrollable forces as the dominating concept in his major work. The urban-minded Kazin, failing to follow up his brilliant comparison of Curtis Jadwin in *The Pit* to "the erring father" in a temperance tract, paid tribute to the exuberance of Norris' writing, but then quickly dismissed the author as an "overgrown boy" with an "indiscriminate" gift. Taylor, more traditionally minded than the others, found inconsistencies in Norris' artistic theories as well as in his economic philosophy, but conceded that he had created "a large, credible, interesting, and significant imaginative world," and had lifted the "romance of economic conflict" from the "subliterary to the literary level."

While Norris was still receiving what Marchand calls "respectful attention," his stock was surely not rising as fast during the 1940's as that of writers like Melville, James, and Faulkner. It is not surprising, of course, that little was written about him during this decade since the war effort curtailed publications and diverted the efforts of young scholars. When the critics returned to their proper duties, however, it seemed that Norris might be relegated to the museum of literary curiosities.

Certainly his work was not freshly interpreted. In the most ambitious book about Norris since Marchand's study, Lars Åhnebrink in 1947 laid the groundwork for his larger study of American naturalism with a plodding and not wholly convincing collection of extended comparisons of particular works of Norris' and Zola's. Malcolm Cowley, whose discerning criticism had sparked the Faulkner revival, failed to do much for Norris when he repeated in the *Sewanee Review* the old bromides about the stylistic and philosophical shortcomings of naturalism. George Snell in *The Shapers of American Fiction* classified Norris as a "realist," repeated the now rather frayed charges of "inconsistency," and dismissed him as a "good groundbreaker" with "a disorderly mind."

No defender of Norris' imagination rose this time to ask with Ernest Marchand, "Which of our writers . . . has greater skill to create the illusion of life?" Norris' stock was at the lowest point it has ever reached, and it looked as if the postwar generation had simply lost interest—as well the war-weary and disillusioned might—in a writer who specialized in violent melodrama and prated about the inevitability of good.

In 1950 Lars Åhnebrink's ponderous study *The Beginnings of Naturalism in American Fiction* added to the author's earlier study of the relationship of Norris and Zola a vast amount of erudition about the theories of the naturalists in Europe and the United States, their techniques, and the influences of writers like Huysmans, Turgenev, and Ibsen upon the movement. Far from stimulating new interest in Norris, however, this meticulous work which stressed the novelist's role as an "experimenter" and "pioneer" appeared to be his scholarly tombstone. On hand to throw dirt into the tomb was Clarence Gohdes, who in "The Facts of Life *versus* Pleasant Reading" (his contribution to Arthur Hobson Quinn's *The Literature of the American People*) talked of Norris' "boyish want of sagacity" and then, with the air of a slightly supercilious father, judged him too immature and naïve to be taken quite seriously.

An appropriate funeral oration was delivered by scholarship's Norman Vincent Peale, Van Wyck Brooks, whose *The Confident Years* contains a charming but inconsequential evocation of Norris and Jack London as figures out of a rowdier, more carefree past. This impression is furthered by Frederick Hoffman, who in *The Modern Novel in America* talks principally of Norris as a naturalist whose techniques are no longer employed in serious fiction but have been revived by the writers of popular, violent "thrillers." The effects of the deceased passed into the hands of those who could assay their origins, and Charles Kaplan began publishing in 1953 his discoveries about the sources Norris had used in obtaining factual details for his work.

In Norris' case, however, one of Poe's principal fears was realized—the burial was premature. The corpse was hardly cold when Maxwell Geismar came forward in a long essay in *Rebels and Ancestors* (1953) with the discovery that Norris was not just a typical product of the confusion of his times but a man whose imagination allowed him to transcend the limitations of his background and training. The wake turned into a revel as a scholarly gang armed with new weapons arrived to disperse the mourners and minimizers. The most productive period in Norris scholarship began in 1955.

The reinterpretation of Norris started just a little too early for all of the studies to benefit from Franklin Walker's invaluable edition of Norris' letters in 1956. Although only fragments of the novelist's correspondence remain, these are enough to enable us to see that the undisciplined energy and enthusiasm of the novels overflowed into the author's private life and also to discover the extreme diffidence which made it almost impossible for Norris to speak without clowning of the things closest to his heart.

Even without the benefit of letters, the critics of the mid-1950's found provocative things to say. Writing in the *South Atlantic Quarterly* in 1955, Charles G. Hoffmann belatedly pointed out what should have long been apparent—that Norris made extensive use of the theme of the regenerative power of love, but that this theme was often obscured by the stylistic effectiveness of the scenes of violent action. Hoffmann points the way to a proper concept of the convictions that really motivated Norris, but he does not appear to have realized that Norris may have obscured his "message" because of his boyish embarrassment about displays of affection and his Victorian qualms about mentioning sex.

A few months later, Donald Pizer, more aware of the sources of Norris' difficulty, pointed out in "Another Look at *The*

Octopus," how the author's theories actually looked not forward but backward to transcendentalism. The next year, Henry Piper, looking in a different direction, related Norris to the twentieth century by pointing out the influence that he had upon Scott Fitzgerald during the years the latter was trying to find his distinctive style. Piper also implicitly condemned the academicians of the first quarter of this century by describing Fitzgerald's anger that he had never been introduced to writers like Norris— who faced problems similar to his own—by professors who shunned "contemporary literature."

By far the most interesting and ambitious work to take a new look at Norris is also the most wrongheaded. In *The Dream of Success*, Kenneth Lynn discusses the effort of five turn-of-the-century novelists (Norris, Dreiser, London, Phillips, Herrick) to adjust the myth of financial success propagated by Horatio Alger to the realities of the world in which they had grown up. Beginning with a brilliant analysis of Dreiser's personal, callous worship of what William James called "the bitch-goddess Success," Lynn has less success with Norris, whose whole career he interprets as an attempt to be recognized as a success by the father who had abandoned him.

Unfortunately, there is not enough evidence of Norris' relations with his father to support the argument; and, in building his case upon Norris' fiction, Lynn makes too many mistakes. Vandover, for example, did not really seduce a girl of his *own* social class; McTeague's loss of his dental practice is not punishment for success, but for crossing Marcus; Norris cannot be identified with Presley in *The Octopus* nor Corthell in *The Pit*, both of whom were the "type" of effete artist he distrusted; and the Jadwin marriage in *The Pit* does not begin to go to pieces *immediately*, but only after the three years during which the couple exhausts each other's slender intellectual resources. Lynn, furthermore, neglects *Blix* altogether and ends his argument with the implausible conclusion that, in *The Pit*, Norris allows his father to best him symbolically. Norris had phobias, but from *Vandover* to *The Octopus* and "Dying Fires" what he fears most is that self-indulgence will destroy his creative powers. Actually, like a good fraternity man, Norris feared anything that made the individual conspicuous, because he saw as one of the principal degenerative forces of commercial civilization, the lionizing which hampered the individual from pursuing his work.

Relations with his father no doubt affected Norris' writing; but rather than trying to impress the older man, Norris seems to have been searching for a symbolic way to minimize the father's success. Having depicted in *The Pit* how a man obviously based upon his father is thoroughly beaten, Norris is then free to make the magnanimous gesture of allowing the defeated man a prospect of future happiness. Norris was very well aware of the dangerous temptations that faced the second generation *nouveau riche*, and he saw safety from them only in an irrational commitment to work for its own sake—not the sake of material reward—a sort of Carlyleism. Norris was an undisciplined thinker, but a far stronger-minded man that Lynn gives him credit for being. Indeed the thing that turns up so often in Norris' work that we suspect it must have come from his observation of his own family, is the superficial culture of a woman who resembles his mother. He seems more interested in browbeating than charming his family; certainly they must have been distressed at the kinds of characters and subjects he chose. Lynn is ingenious, but he is not careful enough about his facts or appreciative enough of Norris' confusion of his private theories with universal truth to construct a convincing argument.

A less fanciful but more perceptive analysis of Norris appeared when he was one of only ten American novelists to catch the attention of another myth-minded critic, Richard Chase. In his *The American Novel and Its Tradition,* we learn that Norris was influenced by "the folklore of Populism," compounded of the "agrarian myth" of a pastoral Golden Age and the Calvinist myth with its emphasis on a "Manichaean demonology." This folklore leads Norris to embrace "the conspiracy theory of history" which I have cited in my preface—"that all would be well with American life if only it were not for the machinations of the money power."

Chase is also the first to assert boldly and convincingly that *The Octopus* is a kind of "subnovel," just as Presley, the poet in it, is a "subintellectual," and Vanamee, the shepherd, a "submystic." Chase, furthermore, is not upset by the stylistic crudities that disturb some critics and is willing to give Norris full credit for "reclaiming for American fiction an imaginative profundity that the Age of Howells was leaving out." Chase's theories accord with the novels far better than Lynn's, and his analysis is one of the soundest ever advanced, but since it is based only on *McTeague* and *The Octopus,* it is not comprehensive enough.

Both Chase's and Lynn's essays are signs that Norris still merits the attention of men who have original ideas about literature, which—whether sound or not—provoke the vigorous controversy that alone can keep criticism flourishing.

Coming between these stimulating re-examinations of Norris, Charles Walcutt's *American Literary Naturalism* is anticlimactic; but "this attempt to determine the exact nature of [Norris'] naturalism and of the ideology which found expression through his work" is invaluable in establishing the philosophical weakness of Norris' thinking and the "intellectual softness" that prevented his mastering a non-teleological philosophy. Walcutt's essay reads like a post mortem, but—along with the *Letters* published in the same year—it lays the groundwork for future study. By the time these books appeared, Norris' reputation as a naturalist had been exploded, but critics were beginning to suppose that he might have been something else. Between Walcutt's essay and Arnold Goldsmith's "The Development of Frank Norris' Philosophy" about all has been said that needs saying about Norris' relationship to deterministic thought and literary naturalism. Some recent essays indicate, however, that there is something else to say.

Stanley Cooperman's "Frank Norris and the Werewolf of Guilt" (1959) develops a theme that Chase barely touches upon and suggests that in his first novels Norris was far more influenced by the Calvinistic concept of guilt than by scientific naturalism. And William B. Dillingham in "Frank Norris and the Genteel Tradition" (1960) impressively documents Norris' strong ties with the polite society he is generally supposed to have been in revolt against. Both essays, as well as George Johnson's less incisive "Frank Norris and Romance" (1961), which deals with the novelist's underlying pastoralism, indicate that the most recent trend in Norris studies is to continue the effort that Chase stimulated to identify the characteristics that link the author to a literary and cultural past. Since Norris has been treated as a youthful rebel for half a century, critics are beginning to feel that it is time to determine his place in the tradition. Perhaps the most important recent essays about Norris are those by Donald Pizer in *PMLA* (December, 1961) and *American Quarterly* (Spring, 1962), which link Norris with "the late nineteenth-

century effort to reconcile evolutionary science and religious
faith."

Strangely enough none of these critics has sufficiently elabo-
rated upon Norris' relationship to the transcendental tradition,
one of the most important in American literature. Although
Donald Pizer briefly connects the two, even he fails to consider
the extent to which Norris—in some ways even more completely
than Whitman—answered Emerson's call for an American poet.
Speaking of the bard for whom he looked in vain, Emerson
wrote: "We do not, with sufficient plainness, or sufficient pro-
foundness, address ourselves to life, nor dare we chaunt our own
times and social circumstances. . . . We have yet had no genius
in America, with tyrannous eye, which knew the value of our
incomparable materials, and saw in the barbarism and materialism of the times, another carnival of the same gods whose picture
he so much admires in Homer."

Whitman had catalogued the things that Emerson demanded
be discussed, but only rarely (as in "The Song of the Redwood
Tree") had he constructed narratives that gave his lyrics the
coherence an epic needs. Certainly Norris chaunted his own
times and circumstances; yet with the tyrannous eye of the
melodramatist interested in subject as well as plot, he made
such fresh use of the incomparable materials that he shocked the
effete as Whitman had with "Children of Adam" and Mark
Twain had with *Huckleberry Finn.*

Surely, too, in the "big scenes" of both *The Octopus* and *The
Pit,* Norris wrote quite consciously of "another carnival of the
same gods" we admire in Homer—even citing parallels. And is it
not the relationship between barbarism and materialism—the
effects of self-indulgence in bringing the brute to the surface—
that preoccupied Norris in all of his major works from *Vandover*
to *The Pit?* Although Norris never even hints that he may be
aware of Emerson's plea, certainly his preservation in his fiction
of the panorama of Polk Street life, of the savage tactics of the
octopoidal railroad, and of polite-society-turned-bestial in *The
Pit* must have been inspired by the same feelings. The bursts of
patriotic fervor in Norris' work show that he would have agreed
that "America is a poem in our eyes." No study of the persistence
of transcendental thought in this country should ignore the
exuberant, undisciplined figure of Frank Norris.

If it has not been sufficiently acknowledged that Norris looks

backward to the first excited flush of transcendentalism, neither
has it been recognized that the pessimistic tone of his writings,
which Chase points out, looks forward to the work of a fellow
Californian, Robinson Jeffers. Although Norris' hatred of civilization never drives him to such extreme statements as Jeffers' poem
"Original Sin" ("I would rather be a worm in a wild apple than
a son of man"), the seeds of the attitude that motivated "Shine,
Perishing Republic" and *Roan Stallion* are found in the Vanamee
story in *The Octopus* and in *McTeague*.

The conclusion of *The Octopus* with its echo of Vanamee's
philosophy that one should abandon the degenerate struggle of
"civilized" people and begin to live in accordance with the
secret rhythms of nature, foreshadows especially the end of
Jeffers' "The Tower Beyond Tragedy," in which Orestes, after
describing how he has renounced all incestuous desires and has
entered into the life of non-human nature, concludes, "I have
fallen in love outward."

What Douglas Bush says about Jeffers—"the peace that passeth
understanding is to be found in a return from 'Civilization, the
enemy of man,' to the earlier fountain, the unconscious life of
earth and air and water (and hawks), the timeless physical
universe which reduces humanity to insignificance"[2]—might have
been said of Norris and the "motes in the sunshine" speech near
the end of *The Octopus*. Bush's conclusion that it is "only too
easy to pigeonhole Mr. Jeffers' type of sentimental primitivism"
as "an example *par excellence* of the nihilistic death-spasms of
the romantic tradition" applies with equal force to Norris.

Bush's mention of nihilism leads to the observation that the
single best criticism of the "type" that Frank Norris represents
was written by a later, British novelist who probably did not
even know the American's work. Joyce Cary's *An American
Visitor* concerns the adventures of a newspaperwoman, Marie
Hasluck, whom another character in the novel describes as:
". . . the real Boston mystic, direct in descent from Emerson and
Thoreau . . . a perfect example of your inner light mystic as
produced so freely by all Protestant nations, especially in times
of trouble. People who despaired of the existing state of things,
and wanted to find a short cut to a new one—and found it by
revelation."[3]

Marie's philosophy is specifically illustrated in a conversation
with the character responsible for the description above. When

Marie announces that a group of African natives are "the happiest kind of people," because they have an education that has "just grown up," the other replies that traditional education has not always produced the best results. Undaunted, Marie replies that the people must be brought up to like "the right kind of things, the natural things." He pounces:

"What are the natural right things . . . who decides what's natural and what isn't? Some kind of a god?"
"Why no, it's just nature." But she was obviously disconcerted. . . .
"Nature or God, it's all the same if it makes the rule. So Birri is really the kingdom of heaven. It doesn't need a government because it's been put on the right lines for ever."[4]

Through the character of Vanamee, Norris argues as Marie does. Cary points out in his introduction to the novel that he was inspired to write it by a young American woman who had told him that Americans believed "children should get their own ideas of right and wrong." Concluding that "it is the essential job of political officers . . . to take responsibility for dodging their own laws or breaking their own rebels," Cary calls a person who thinks like this young woman, "an anarchist of the most extreme kind."[5]

McTeague with its implicit denunciation of professional licensing and its condemnation of money because some people make a fetish of it, *Moran* and *A Man's Woman* with their unabashed praise of power and impulse, *The Octopus* with its shepherd whose "sixth sense" makes him superior to other men —all these show that an anarchist (at least a philosophical one) is exactly what Norris is. Hatred of civilization, although one may not realize it, is a yearning for anarchy—for allowing every man the unrestricted right to pursue good after his own fashion. The assumption that good is to be found in some kind of non-intellectual "natural" order merely allows the anarchist to pass the buck for his own lack of discipline, since there can be as many "natural orders" as there are men clever enough to set up their own behavior as an absolute good.

The frontier and the free enterprise society of nineteenth-century America not only permitted but encouraged anarchy. The Agrarian and American Success myths allowed Norris to believe that problems could be universally solved in the way that the very special conditions of his childhood allowed them to be solved. In his insistence on clinging to these myths and in his nearly hysterical warnings against the growth of an increasingly urbanized society to which such myths might prove inapplicable, he did indeed—as his most astute critics have suggested—look not forward to an age that would be the beneficiary of social reform but backward to a supposed age of innocence when there was no need for reform.

What the curious link he provides between the benignly optimistic Emerson and the mordantly pessimistic Jeffers shows is what a century of mechanized civilization had done to transcendentalism. Thoreau's experimental retreat to Walden Pond had become Jeffers' permanent retreat into his castle by the sea, and the impatience with "quiet desperation" had turned into a rejection of the kind of degenerate selfishness symbolized by incest. Norris stands exactly on the point where the nineteenth-century faith in the eventual triumph of good curdles into the twentieth-century despair at the continued persistence of evil. If the novelist had lived longer, he might have been tempted to precede Jeffers into isolation in some California fastness where he could rail unmolested at unheeding humanity.

The trouble with transcendentalist thinkers has always been that in their well-motivated eagerness to escape the destructive pedantry of books and the conformity imposed by traditionalism, they have been too prone to put their faith in some sort of secret cosmic order that one participates in by *doing* and *feeling* (like a fraternity initiation) rather than *thinking*, without realizing that—as depicted in *The Octopus* and *The Grapes of Wrath*—when groups with feelings of cosmically ordained righteousness conflict, destructive violence results.

Norris' shortcoming was that he had too little knowledge of the workings of the Nature that he praised excessively and too little confidence in man's ability to discipline himself and bounce back from disaster; thus he could not be objective about human irresponsibility—except fleetingly in "A Deal in Wheat" and *The Pit*. Yet despite this shortcoming, Norris' works have permanent value.

I began this book with the observation that this novelist is best understood as a fraternity man—a refugee from intellectualism. Our schools—our whole world, in fact, is full of such refugees—perpetual undergraduates in a society that needs the kind of minds college training *should* develop.[6] If such people can be led to read at all, they can identify with Norris' attitudes as they cannot with those of a more intellectually mature writer. Finding their own beliefs, prejudices and fears embodied in his writing, they begin to see that literature is really about them.

The danger is, of course, that discovering such literature will only confirm beliefs that these readers should be beginning to outgrow. Here the teacher or critic faces his great challenge. If he can lead such readers first to recognize themselves in such books and then to discern the shortcomings of the philosophy underlying this work, he may be able to start them on the road toward "the examined life." This difficult effort is worth while, since it is unlikely that those who never read critically can ever lead other than the "unexamined life" Socrates condemns, while even those who cannot progress beyond Norris' "romantic anarchism" will feel less alone in a hostile world after reading him.

Norris' works are thus valuable not only in the study of American literature, but in themselves. Through the books commonly recognized as his best—*McTeague, The Octopus, The Pit*—we can, to the accompaniment of exciting stories, observe how a man who started out as a frightened, sentimental primitivist was led at last to the brink of a reconciliation with civilization. If we fail to recognize, however, that *The Pit* does crown Norris' career, we fail to see how much progress he made toward artistic and philosophical maturity during his brief career.

For a rounded understanding of Norris, we should read along with his best works the slight but unjustly neglected *Blix,* which shows just what the novelist expected of the civilization that so often depressed and disgusted him. His other works we may justifiably neglect; yet we must still be struck by the amount accomplished in a single decade by a writer who was just achieving intellectual maturity when he died. How many have written even four novels in the tractarian tradition that bring both the physical atmosphere and the thinking of an important past era back to life? Thousands of dead tracts moulder in libraries beside thousands of purely escapist fantasies; but only a few writers have had the combination of characteristics that enabled Norris to fuse melodrama and morality into stories that make readers both able and willing to project themselves into an era that did much to shape—and misshape—our modern urban society.

Notes and References

Chapter One

1. Franklin Walker, *Frank Norris* (Garden City, N. Y., 1932), p. 60.
2. But like other bored and rebellious students, he may have learned more than he realized from his instructors. Donald Pizer, "Evolutionary Ethical Dualism in Frank Norris' *Vandover and the Brute* and *McTeague*" (*PMLA*, LXXVI, 552-60, 1961) discusses the possible influence upon Norris of his science teacher, Joseph Le Conte.
3. Walker, *Frank Norris*, p. 291.
4. "Fact into Ficton in *McTeague*," *Harvard Library Bulletin*, VIII, 381-85 (Autumn, 1954).
5. See especially his diatribe against a boy who worked nine years to win a Townsend Prize at Yale ("Salt and Sincerity," *Collected Works*, VII, 200-4).
6. Wallace Everett, "Frank Norris in His Chapter," *The Phi Gamma Delta*, LII, 561 (April, 1930).
7. Franklin Walker, "An Early Frank Norris Item," *Book Club of California Quarterly News Letter*, XXV, 83-86 (Fall, 1960).
8. Everett, "Frank Norris in His Chapter," p. 566.
9. Channing Pollock, *Harvest of My Years, An Autobiography* (Indianapolis, 1943), p. 73.
10. *Frank Norris of the Wave* (San Francisco, 1931), p. 219.
11. Norris discusses his impression of Howells in a letter to Mrs. Elizabeth H. Davenport, March 12, 1898 (reprinted in *The Letters of Frank Norris*, p. 6). It is not accurate to suggest, as some critics do, that Norris differs from Howells in his use of violence, since there is considerable physical violence in Howells' *The Landlord at Lion's Head*, published the year before the two novelists met. Norris probably went further than Howells thought he should go himself; but if the younger man had really gone too far to suit Howells, the older would have probably treated Norris as Emerson did Whitman.
12. Franklin Walker (ed.), *The Letters of Frank Norris* (San Francisco, 1956), p. 51.
13. Paul H. Bixler, "Frank Norris' Literary Reputation," *American Literature*, VI, 109-21 (May, 1934). In the original trade editions *Moran* sold 1,804 copies; *McTeague*, 3,974; *Blix*, 4,076; *A Man's Woman*, 5,334. *The Pit* sold more than all others combined, 94,818.
14. In 1899 Norris complained to a San Francisco friend that he could not become accustomed to the East and that he hoped to return

West when he had established connections. Walker (ed.) *Letters of Frank Norris,* p. 31.

15. Walker, *Frank Norris,* p. 282.

16. *Ibid.,* p. 286.

17. *Greed* is one of the most highly acclaimed pictures of all time, even though it was released only in a drastically cut version. It was, however, a financial failure and ended Von Stroheim's career as a director. For a discussion of the making of the film and its relation to the novel see Arthur Knight, *The Liveliest Art* (New York, 1957), pp. 138-42.

Chapter Two

1. "His Sister," *Frank Norris of the Wave,* p. 34.

2. I imply here that Pope and Emerson had a similar concept of a universal, "natural" order, although they had quite different ideas about how the individual might gain knowledge of it. As these two arch-representatives indicate, the quarrel between the classical and romantic viewpoints concerned principally means not ends. Jacques Barzun in *Classic, Romantic, and Modern* (New York: Anchor Books, 1961; pp. 87-88) makes the distinction between the two viewpoints most clear when he explains: "The lesson of Descartes can presumably be learned from reading . . . the *Discourse on Method.* Descartes has alone done the perilous work. . . . The lesson that Faust learns can only be found in the undergoing of experience itself." The essence of the classical view (which Emerson attacks in "Self-Reliance") is that man learns by example; the essence of the transcendentalist romantic viewpoint is that he learns by experience. Both accept the idea of a universal order, as does Norris.

3. Willard E. Martin, "Two Uncollected Essays by Frank Norris," *American Literature,* VIII, 190-91 (May, 1936). This essay might have been omitted from collections of Norris' work because of editorial fears that its outspokenness might offend southerners.

4. Richard Chase, *The American Novel and Its Tradition,* Anchor Books Edition (Garden City, N. Y., 1957), p. 191. The observation is truer of Norris' theories than of his work. Had he not really been interested in people, his novels would probably be lifeless hulks. His remarks about Harriet Beecher Stowe suggest that he could not even understand how a writer could generate enough enthusiasm for a "cause" to keep him working.

Chapter Three

1. The brief scene of Vandover sitting in his back yard playing with guinea pigs (p. 3) could, for example, be developed into an effective foreshadowing of the concluding scene in which the small

boy watches Vandover clean out the mess from under the sink (p. 311). As the scene from Vandover's childhood now stands, it adds nothing to the novel; but Norris may have jotted it down for later development.

2. See the Preface and Introduction to the novel in *Collected Works* for their comments.

3. At least one specific agent of civilization is attacked in this novel, although without a word of direct criticism. Although there is no preaching in Chapter Nine, the gripping description of the shipwreck and its aftermath is an effective exposure of the wretched conditions on second-class ships that foreshadows the technique Norris will use in dealing with the railroad in *The Octopus*.

Chapter Four

1. Ernest Marchand, *Frank Norris, A Study* (Stanford University, c. 1942), pp. 65-66.

2. S. I. Hayakawa, *Language in Thought and Action* (New York, c. 1949), p. 197. Significantly, the distinction is made in a discussion of anti-Semitism. Norris' attitude towards Jews is probably itself attributable to the very suspicion of the "symbol-handler" that Hayakawa discusses.

3. Ernest Marchand, in *Frank Norris, A Study*, attributes Norris' use of primitive types to a positive worship of brawniness; it is at least equally possible that the exaltation of "red-bloodedness" at the turn of the century was a negative reaction to the intellectual demands of an increasingly technological society. The continued rural preference for football players over laboratory workers stems partly from the ability of the unsophisticated to understand phyiscal action only.

4. The "thing-handler" need not move to the city to get into trouble with "symbol-handlers." *The Grapes of Wrath* is basically about the expulsion of primitive agrarian "thing-handlers" by the "symbol-handlers" from the banks, but even here the source of evil is the city—the foreclosures are "orders from the East."

5. Charles G. Hoffmann, "Norris and the Responsibility of the Novelist," *South Atlantic Quarterly*, LIV, 508-15 (October, 1955). Hoffmann writes one of the most perceptive analyses of the moral code underlying Norris' books, but he makes too much of the author's affirmative moments and fails to recognize his almost hysterical rejection of the "unnatural."

6. H. M. Wright, "In Memoriam—Frank Norris," *University of California Chronicle*, V, 240-45 (October, 1902).

7. Walker, *Frank Norris*, p. 278.

8. An example of the holding action of the "thing-handlers" is

the freezing of many state legislatures into patterns of representation established in 1900 or 1910 before the power of the cities, home of the "symbol manipulators," became so pronounced that it threatened to destroy the power of the then dominant rural communities. These anachronistic patterns of representation have just begun to be seriously challenged by federal court decisions in 1962.

Chapter Five

1. *Collected Works*, Vol. IX, p. ix, "*Moran of the Lady Letty* grew out of Frank's desire to stage a physical fight between a man and a woman." He was preoccupied with such matters when he wrote *McTeague*, too. Since then—as G. Legman points out in *Love and Death* (1949)—such behavior has become a staple of the most vicious comic books. Norris' anti-intellectualism makes him the predecessor of some of the trashiest writers of our century, whose cynical lack of moral fervor would probably dismay him.

2. Walker (ed.), *Letters of Frank Norris*, p. 6.

3. Norris has a spokesman enlarge upon just what a good girl can do in "The Opinions of Leander," published in *The Wave* in July and August, 1897, and collected in *Frank Norris of the Wave*. In these essays he several times repeats a condemnation of men's drinking at parties and of young girls' smoking anywhere. Just how completely adolescent Norris remained at twenty-seven is shown by his quoting favorably a man who glares fiercely at another when his "girl's" name is brought up. They agree "never to talk of a good, straight girl among themselves; say nothing about her good, bad, or indifferent" (*Frank Norris of the Wave*, p. 250). Unless the sketches are satirical—and there is no evidence that they are—Norris certainly may be called "prissy." His own extremely puritanical behavior is another evidence that his sensational fiction was his way of striking back at the civilization he detested.

4. In *The Octopus* (II, 245), Norris becomes even more vehement against the women's clubs and literary organizations because of the amount of time and money they waste on a colorful assortment of "fakes."

5. Quoted by Daniel Lang in the *New Yorker*, July 22, 1961, p. 63.

6. Grant Knight, *The Strenuous Age in American Literature* (Chapel Hill, North Carolina, 1954), p. 35.

7. Much is omitted here, including a dozen uses of the word *American*. Norris tries as hard to convince himself and the reader as the committee does to convince Ward. These men of action are extremely long-winded.

8. Walker (ed.), *Letters of Frank Norris*, p. 48.
9. Miss Tompkins discusses Norris' views in her nostalgic foreword to *The Pit*. Collected Edition, Vol. IX, pp. ix-x.

Chapter Six

1. This interpretation is fostered by an abridgement like that in Blair, Hornberger, and Stewart's *The Literature of the United States*, revised edition, II, 618-39, which reproduces only those passages dealing with the struggle between the ranchers and the railroad.
2. Walker, *The Letters of Frank Norris*, p. 41. He invites her to present her side.
3. H. Willard Reninger, "Norris Explains *The Octopus*: A Correlation of His Theory and Practice," *American Literature*, XII, 225 (May, 1940).
4. The historical background of this novel and of other works dealing with the same incident is explained in Irving McKee's "Notable Memorials to Mussel Slough," *Pacific Historical Review*, XVII, 19-27 (February, 1948).
5. Donald Pizer, "Another Look at *The Octopus*," *Nineteenth-Century Fiction*, X, 224 (December, 1955).
6. Walker (ed.), *The Letters of Frank Norris*, p. 67.
7. *The Grapes of Wrath* (New York, 1939), pp. 50-51. In this chapter, Steinbeck attributes to the bankers and their agents who are dispossessing the sharecroppers, the same rationalizations Shelgrim uses to exonerate himself.

Chapter Seven

1. William B. Dillingham, "Frank Norris and the Genteel Tradition," *Tennessee Studies in Literature*, V, 15-24 (1960). Jadwin still cannot discuss anything about his relations with his wife with others. His attitude is that of the embarrassed juvenile in "The Opinions of Leander" (*Frank Norris of the Wave*, pp. 220-50). As his inability to stop speculating also shows, although he is a "self-made man," he is still emotionally adolescent.

Chapter Eight

1. Arnold Louis Goldsmith, "The Development of Frank Norris' Philosophy," *Studies in Honor of John Wilcox* (Detroit, 1958), pp. 175-94.

Chapter Nine

1. Contemporary reviews of Norris' novels are analyzed at length in Ernest Marchand's *Frank Norris, A Study* (Palo Alto, c. 1942), pp. 175-94.

Notes and References

2. Douglas Bush, *Mythology and the Romantic Tradition in English Poetry* (New York, 1957), p. 522.

3. Joyce Cary, *An American Visitor* (New York, n. d.), p. 151. Although not published in the United States until 1961, the novel was originally issued in England in 1932.

4. *Ibid.*, pp. 89-90.

5. *Ibid.*, pp. 243-47.

6. The confused values of these men is illustrated by Norris' being upset about the "bad form" of using hotel stationery, yet lying about his birth and education to a stranger who had praised his work. (Walker, ed., *The Letters of Frank Norris*, pp. 5, 22: Norris claims to have been born in California and to have graduated from Harvard.)

Selected Bibliography

PRIMARY SOURCES

A seven-volume collected "Golden Gate" edition of 1903 was superseded in 1928 by a ten-volume set published by Doubleday, Doran and Company, Garden City, New York. This edition appeared in two formats. The Argonaut Manuscript Limited Edition (245 sets) was bound in simulated vellum and included a page of the original manuscript of *McTeague*, bound into the first volume. The Complete Edition was identical with the Argonaut, except that it was bound in black cloth and contained no manuscript. Although dated 1928, it did not appear until the next year.

All references throughout this book are to the latter edition, which contains:

Volumes I and II, *The Octopus* (originally published in 1901), with a foreword by Irvin S. Cobb in Volume I.

Volume III, *Blix* (originally published in 1899), pp. 1-174, with an introduction by Kathleen Norris; and *Moran of the Lady Letty* (originally published in 1898), pp. 177-326, with an introduction by Rupert Hughes.

Volume IV, *The Third Circle* (short stories—originally published in 1909), pp. 1-165; and *A Deal in Wheat and Other Stories of the New and Old West* (originally published in 1903), pp. 171-332, with an introduction to both by Will Irwin.

Volume V, *Vandover and the Brute* (originally published in 1914), with a foreword by Charles Norris and an introduction by H. L. Mencken.

Volume VI, *A Man's Woman* (originally published in 1900), pp. 1-245, with a foreword by Christopher Morley; and *Yvernelle* (originally published in 1891), pp. 248-314.

Volume VII, *The Responsibilities of the Novelist* (critical essays—originally published in 1903), pp. 3-226, with an introduction, "Frank Norris; or, Up from Culture," by Charles Caldwell Dobie, and a foreword by Grant Overton; and *The Joyous Miracle* (short story—originally published in 1897), pp. 229-36.

Volume VIII, *McTeague* (originally published in 1899), with an introduction by Theodore Dreiser.

Volume IX, *The Pit* (originally published in 1903), with a foreword by Juliet Wilbor Tompkins.

Volume X, *Collected Writings Hitherto Unpublished in Book Form*, with an introduction by Charles Norris. (Contains selections from the San Francisco *Wave* and the *Overland Monthly*, South African and Spanish-American War reports, and three later short stories.)

This edition is not complete. Other writings of Norris' are found in:

Two Poems and "Kim" Reviewed. San Francisco: Harvey Taylor, 1930. Unpaged.

Frank Norris of "The Wave" with a foreword by Charles Norris and an introduction by Oscar Lewis. San Francisco: The Westgate Press, 1931. 250pp. (Stories and sketches published in the San Francisco weekly between 1893 and 1897.)

MARTIN, WILLARD E. (ed.) "Two Uncollected Essays by Frank Norris," *American Literature*, VIII, 190-98 (May, 1936).

WALKER, FRANKLIN, (ed.) *The Letters of Frank Norris.* San Francisco: Book Club of California, 1956. 99pp.

————, (ed.) "An Early Frank Norris Item," *Book Club of California Quarterly News Letter*, XXV, 83-86 (Fall, 1960).

SECONDARY SOURCES

LOHF, KENNETH and EUGENE P. SHEEHY, *Frank Norris: A Bibliography.* Los Gatos, California: Talisman Press, 1959. 107pp. (Contains a complete listing of first editions, reprints, translations, and contributions to periodicals; it also lists reviews of Norris' works and writings about Norris. With William White, "Frank Norris: Bibliographical Addenda," *Bulletin of Bibliography*, XIII, 227-28 [September-December, 1959], this supersedes all earlier bibliographies of Norris' work.)

There is no anthology of Norris criticisms. The articles listed below are candidates for such a volume. For other criticisms, see the Lohf and Sheehy bibliography listed above.

I. *Biographies*

WALKER, FRANKLIN. *Frank Norris, A Biography.* Garden City: Doubleday, Doran, 1932. The only full-length study of the novelist's life. The biographer is uncritical of his subject, but the book is extraordinarily detailed and contains much valuable information drawn from personal interviews with Norris' friends and family.

     *   *   *   *

EVERETT, WALLACE W. "Frank Norris in His Chapter." The *Phi Gamma Delta*, LII, 561-66 (April, 1930). Describes Norris' undergraduate high jinks and contains a valuable portrait and other illustrations.

HART, JAMES D. "Search and Research: The Librarian and the Scholar," *College and Research Libraries*, XIX, 365-74 (September, 1958). A fascinating account of the effort to reassemble the manuscript of *McTeague* and to bring Norris' books and papers together in the Bancroft Library of the University of California.

MARTIN, WILLARD E. "Frank Norris' Reading at Harvard College," *American Literature*, VII, 203-4 (May, 1935). Lists the books he withdrew from the library in the spring of 1895.

PEIXOTTO, ERNEST. "Romanticist Under the Skin," *Saturday Review of Literature*, IX, 613-15 (May 27, 1933). An invaluable account —illustrated with some of Norris' sketches—of his life as an art student in San Francisco and Paris, by one of his closest friends.

WRIGHT, H. M. "In Memoriam—Frank Norris," *University of California Chronicle*, V, 240-45 (October, 1902). An intimate description of the college days of "an ideal club man" by an undergraduate friend.

II. *General Criticisms*

MARCHAND, ERNEST LEROY. *Frank Norris, A Study*. California: Stanford University Press, c. 1942. A detailed study that endeavors "to place Norris against the wider background of his period—social and intellectual as well as purely literary—to examine the several aspects of his thought and of his work, and to take stock of critical opinion about him from his own day to the present."

●   ●   ●   ●

CARGILL, OSCAR. *Intellectual America*. New York: MacMillan, 1941, pp. 89-107. Contains a succinct, intelligent account of Norris' artistic strengths and weaknesses in relation to the whole naturalistic movement.

CHAMBERLAIN, JOHN. *Farewell to Reform*. New York: Liveright, c. 1932, pp. 104-10. Observes that Norris shared the prejudices, the unconscious morals, the values of the "ascendant middle-class," but finds this regrettable.

CHASE, RICHARD VOLNEY. "Norris and Naturalism," *The American Novel and Its Tradition*. Garden City, N. Y.: Doubleday Anchor Books, 1957, pp. 185-204. Discusses *McTeague* and *The Octopus* as continuations of an earlier American literary tradition under the new guise of naturalism.

COOPER, FREDERIC TABER. *Some American Story Tellers*. New York: Henry Holt, 1911, pp. 295-330. An accurate, spirited appraisal of Norris' accomplishments by one of his first critics.

Selected Bibliography

COOPERMAN, STANLEY. "Frank Norris and the Werewolf of Guilt," *Modern Language Quarterly*, XX, 252-58 (September, 1959). Argues that in *McTeague* and *Vandover*, Norris' commitment to scientific determinism is simply verbally superimposed upon the Calvinist belief that instinct is evil.

DILLINGHAM, WILLIAM B. "Frank Norris and the Genteel Tradition," *Tennessee Studies in Literature*, V, 15-24 (1960). Shows how, in Norris' treatment of sex as vice and of the moral influence of women, he had close ties with the genteel tradition he supposedly revolted against.

GEISMAR, MAXWELL. "Frank Norris: and the Brute." *Rebels and Ancestors*. Boston: Houghton Mifflin, 1953, pp. 3-66. Discusses the extent to which Norris "had come away from the typical standards and superstitions of his youthful background, as well as from the destructive elements in his own temperament" and stresses his similarity to Scott Fitzgerald as a chronicler of the dissolute society of his era.

GOHDES, CLARENCE L. F. "Facts of Life *versus* Pleasant Reading," *The Literature of the American People*. Edited by Arthur H. Quinn. New York: Appleton-Century-Crofts, 1951, pp. 749-54. An acerb account that grants the unusual scope and energy of *McTeague* and *The Octopus*, but finds Norris generally immature and too naïve to be taken quite seriously.

GOLDSMITH, ARNOLD LOUIS. "The Development of Frank Norris' Philosophy," *Studies in Honor of John Wilcox*. Detroit: Wayne State University Press, 1958, pp. 174-94. Outlines four stages in the development of Norris' philosophy leading to his view that "though man may frequently be the victim of chance, heredity, environment, and life itself, mankind evolves steadily upward, and good will ultimately prevail."

HOFFMAN, FREDERICK J. *The Modern Novel in America*. Gateway Edition. Chicago: Regnery, c. 1956, pp. 31-44. Provides an analysis with illustrations from Norris of the problems of organization and characterization facing the naturalistic novelist.

HOFFMANN, CHARLES G. "Norris and the Responsibility of the Novelist," *South Atlantic Quarterly*, LIV, 508-15 (October, 1955). Shows how "the power of love as man's saving force in an impersonal world" runs through Norris' work and is most successfully developed in *The Pit*, so that his work reflects not steady artistic development, but a movement from a negative to a positive concept of a moral nature that raises man above the brute.

HOWELLS, WILLIAM DEAN. "Frank Norris," *North American Review*, CLXXV, 769-78 (December, 1902). A memorial tribute in which Norris' most influential literary supporter summarizes his earlier criticisms and identifies *McTeague* and *The Octopus* as complementary personal and social epics.

JOHNSON, GEORGE W. "Frank Norris and Romance," *American Literature*, XXXIII, 52-63, (March, 1961). Concerns Norris' attempts to reconstitute romance in American fiction, but does not point out that the idea of the destructive force of the city observable in *McTeague* also permeates all of Norris' later work.

KAZIN, ALFRED. *On Native Grounds*. Anchor Books Edition. Garden City, N. Y.: Doubleday, 1956, pp. 74-79. Discusses Norris as the literary counterpart of the "tough men" of the new century—Theodore Roosevelt, Borah, Darrow.

LYNN, KENNETH S. "Frank Norris: Mama's Boy," *Dream of Success: A Study of the Modern American Imagination*. Boston: Little, Brown, c. 1955, pp. 158-207. An ingenious but shaky picture of Norris as a weakling torn between his parents and who wrote his novels in an attempt to impress his father.

PATTEE, FRED LEWIS. *A History of American Literature Since 1870*. New York: Century, 1915, pp. 398-400. Epitomizes the early conservative view that recognizes the epic pretension of the Wheat books, but regards them as essentially well-done journalism.

PIPER, HENRY DAN. "Frank Norris and Scott Fitzgerald," *Huntington Library Quarterly*, XIX, 393-400 (August, 1956). Describes Fitzgerald's enthusiasm for Norris and the influence of *Vandover and the Brute* on *The Beautiful and the Damned*.

SPILLER, ROBERT ERNEST. *Cycle of American Literature*. Signet Edition. New York: New American Library, 1957, pp. 154-57. Regards *The Octopus*—"the most ambitious American novel since *Moby Dick*—as a "new kind of primitive epic" historically important because of the author's overreaching his limits.

WALCUTT, CHARLES CHILD. "Frank Norris and the Search for Form," *American Literary Naturalism, A Divided Stream*. Minneapolis: University of Minnesota Press, c. 1956, pp. 114-56. An attempt to determine the nature of Norris' naturalism and of the ideology that finds expression through his work. Walcutt points out the lack of any concrete philosophical basis for Norris' work and introduces the term "mystical natural dynamism" to describe the novelist's theories.

III. *Discussions of The Octopus*

This is the only work of Norris' which has received noteworthy separate attention from analytical critics.

Selected Bibliography

LYNN, KENNETH S. "Introduction" to *The Octopus*. Riverside Edition. Boston: Houghton Mifflin, 1958, pp. v-xxv. Relates the portrayal of Annixter, Presley, and Vanamee to other fictional portrayals of the individual loneliness that has provided one of the most significant themes in distinguished American fiction.

MEYER, GEORGE WILBUR. "A New Interpretation of *The Octopus*," *College English*, IV, 351-59 (March, 1943). Straightens out erroneous conceptions about Norris' attitude toward his characters and points out that, since he did not confuse determinism with fatalism, he did not believe reform impossible.

PIZER, DONALD. "Another Look at *The Octopus*," *Nineteenth-Century Fiction*, X, 217-24 (December, 1955). Shows how the inconsistencies of the novel disappear if it is read as depicting Presley's progress toward the truth that the individual is free to work toward reconciliation with cosmic goodness. (See also Pizer's "The Concept of Nature in Frank Norris' *The Octopus*," *American Quarterly*, XIV, 73-80 [Spring, 1962].)

RENINGER, H. WILLARD. "Norris Explains *The Octopus*: A Correlation of His Theory and Practice," *American Literature*, XII, 218-27 (May, 1940). An analysis of the theories set forth in *The Responsibilities of the Novelist* and their exemplification in *The Octopus*, in which the events "culminate within the consciousness of the reader a single dramatic effect."

IV. Source Studies

AHNEBRINK, LARS. *The Beginnings of Naturalism in American Fiction*. The American Institute in the University of Upsala Essays and Studies on American Language and Literature Number 9. Upsala, Sweden, and Cambridge, Massachusetts: Lundequistska Bokhandeln, c. 1950, 505pp. An exhaustive study of the rise of naturalism in Europe and the United States, the theories and methods of the naturalists, and the influence of Zola, Huysmans, Turgenev, and Ibsen upon Norris. It supersedes the author's earlier *The Influence of Emile Zola upon Frank Norris* (Upsala, 1947).

●　　●　　●　　●

KAPLAN, CHARLES. "Fact into Fiction in *McTeague*," *Harvard Library Bulletin*, VIII, 381-85 (Autumn, 1954). Illustrates that Norris made use of technical material from Thomas Fillebrown's *A Text-Book of Operative Dentistry*.

————. "Norris' Use of Sources in *The Pit*," *American Literature*, XXV, 75-84 (March, 1953). Shows how Norris used and altered the sequence of events in Joseph Leiter's attempt to corner the wheat market in 1897-98, in order to obtain the dramatic effect he desired.

McKEE, IRVING. "Notable Memorials to Mussel Slough," *Pacific Historical Review*, XII, 19-27 (February, 1948). Discusses the actual incident on May 11, 1880, its portrayal in Josiah Royce's only novel *The Feud at Oakfield Creek* (1887), and the influence of *The Octopus* on Theodore Roosevelt.

SHERWOOD, JOHN C. "Norris and the *Jeannette*," *Philological Quarterly*, XXXVII, 245-52 (April, 1958). Traces the detailed descriptions of Arctic exploration in *A Man's Woman* to the published accounts of the disaster of the ship "Jeannette" in 1881.

Index

Ahnebrink, Lars, *The Beginnings of Naturalism in American Fiction*, 132

"Aida of the Coal Mines," 29

Alger, Horatio, and his theories of the "self-made man," 64, 100, 139, 146

Anglo-Saxon Superiority, Theory of, 28, 39-40, 41, 77

Annixter (character in *The Octopus*), 21, 32, 44, 93, 104

Anti-intellectualism, 75, 131, 140-41, 144-45

Anti-Semitism, 69, 71, 144

Argonaut, 31

Arthur, Timothy Shay, *Ten Nights in a Bar-room*, 57, 69

Ashe, Mr. and Mrs. Gaston, 29

Atherton, Gertrude, 125

Barzun, Jacques, *Classic, Romantic, and Modern*, 143

Beach, Joseph Warren, 130

Big Dipper Mine, Colfax, California, 27

Blood: Decadent Spanish, 40-41, 120; Peasant, 69

Boer War, 25

Bougainville Island, 40

Bouguereau, Adolphe, 23, 112

Brady, William A., 32

Brooks, Van Wyck, *The Confident Years*, 132

Burgess, Gelett, 26, 31

Bush, Douglas, 138

California Literary Research Project, 131

Calverton, V. F., *The Liberation of American Literature*, 130

Canary as "alter ego" of McTeague, 67, 74, 75

Cargill, Oscar, *Intellectual America*, 131

Carlyleism, 135

Cary, Joyce, *An American Visitor*, 138-39; *The Horse's Mouth*, 127

Cedarquist (character in *The Octopus*), 101, 107

Chase, Richard, *The American Novel and Its Tradition*, 44, 72, 135-36, 138

Childhood idealized, 47, 59

City (Norris' hatred of), 47, 60, 62, 70-71, 72, 122, 124, 140, 141

Civilization, 51, 59-61, 66-67, 73-75, 78, 97-98, 101, 134, 138-39, 141-45

Conrad, Joseph, 63, 105

"Conspiracy Theory of History," preface, 135

Cooper, Frederic Taber, *Some American Story Tellers*, 128

Cooperman, Stanley, 136

Cosgrave, John O'Hara, 26

Cowley, Malcolm, 132

Crane, Stephen, 28, 102, 105, 128

Critic, 36

Cuba, 28, 77, 117

Dante, 105

Davenport, Mrs. Elizabeth H., 77, 142

Davis, Richard Harding, 28, 131

Del Monte Hotel, 26

Depression of the 1930's, 90, 130-31

Derrick, Magnus (character in *The Octopus*), 92-93, 99-100, 106

Determinism, 30, 59, 90

Deus ex Machina, use of, 82, 85, 103

Dillingham, William B., 65, 113, 136

Dobie, Charles Caldwell, 129

Doubleday, Mr. and Mrs. Frank, 29

Dreiser, Theodore, 68, 107, 130; *An American Tragedy*, 61; *Sister Carrie*, 29, 30, 48

Eliot, George, 25

Emerson, Ralph Waldo, 35, 38, 39, 43, 81, 140, 142, 143; "The Poet," 137

Escapism, 47-48, 141
Everybody's, 119, 125

"Faking," 81, 86-87
Faulkner, William, *Light in August*, 67
"Feeling (or Doing) vs. Thinking," 21, 46, 65, 78, 79-80, 83, 84, 88, 92, 105-6, 117, 140
Fitzgerald, F. Scott, 134
Florence, Italy, 23
Football, 21, 22, 24, 26
Fort Point Coast Guard Station, 27
Frank Norris (motorship), 34
Frank Norris of the Wave, 37 119
Froissart's *Chronicles*, 23
Frontier psychology, 104-5

Gaer, Joseph, 131
Garland, Hamlin, 31, 127
"Gaston le Fox," 23
Gates, Lewis E., 25, 52
Geismar, Maxwell, *Rebels and Ancestors*, 82, 95, 133
George, Henry, 89
Gibbs, George, 30
Gohdes, Clarence, 132
Goldsmith, Arnold, 121, 136
Gothicism, 49-51, 68
Greed, 33, 68, 143

Hagerty's Saloon, 24
Hardy, Thomas, 38, 70
Harrington, Colonel, 31
Harvard *Advocate*, 25
Harvard University, 20, 25, 44, 51
Hathorn, Ralph, 24
Hayakawa, S. I., *Language in Thought and Action*, 72, 144
Hicks, Granville, *The Great Tradition*, 90, 130
Hodgson, Capt. Joseph, 27, 29
Hoffmann, Charles, 73, 109, 133
Hoffman, Frederick J., *The Modern Novel in America*, 133
Homer, 104-5, 128
Hooven Family (characters in *The Octopus*), 62, 93, 102
Howells, William Dean, 28, 29, 31, 109, 112, 123, 127-28, 135; *A Hazard of New Fortunes*, 64; *The Landlord at Lion's Head*, 142; *The Rise of Silas Lapham*, 109, 123
Humbert, Madame, 43
Huntington, Collis, 26, 94, 101
Hutchins, Robert, 44
Huysmans, Karl, 132

Ibsen, Henrik, 132
Investment, Principles of, 72-74, 107-8

James Henry, 46, 63, 128; "The Art of Fiction," 45; *The Bostonians*, 64, 110
James, William, 134
Jameson Raid, 25-26
Jeffers, Robinson, 138, 140
Johnson, George, 136
Julien Atelier, 23

Kaplan, Charles, 20, 133
Kazin, Alfred, 131
Kipling, Rudyard, 82, 120, 131
Knight, Grant, 84, 130

Lackaye, Wilton, 32
Lawlor, Dr. William, 31
LeConte, Joseph, 142
Legman. G., *Love and Death*, 145
Leiter, Joseph, 108
Lewis, Oscar, 33
Lewisohn, Ludwig, *Expression in America*, 130
Licensing (an "unnatural" practice), 62, 73, 139
Life's Whirlpool (movie version of *McTeague*), 32
London, Jack, 31, 131-32
Lycanthropy, 53, 55, 56
Lynn, Kenneth, *The Dream of Success*, 134

Madison Avenue, 105
Marchand, Ernest, *Frank Norris: A Study*, 56, 67, 89, 94, 100, 109, 119, 126, 127, 131, 132
Marcosson, Isaac, 29, 76, 87, 97, 127
Markham, Edwin, 29, 92, 95

Index

Mather, Cotton, 56
McClure, S. S., and *McClure's Magazine*, 27, 29, 76, 90
Mencken, Henry L., 56
Mephistopheles, 103
Meyer, George, 91-92, 96, 131
Milton, 105
Modjeska, Helena, 109
Moody, Dwight L., 23
Moulson, George, 30, 74
"Muckraking," 89-90
Mussel Slough Affair, 29, 92, 146
"Mystic Dynamic Naturalism," 41
Mysticism, 97, 140

Naturalism, 36, 48, 50, 128, 132
Nazism, 40
"New England Spirit," 108, 110
Nihilism, 138
Norris, Benjamin Franklin, Sr. (father), 21, 22, 23, 25, 134
Norris, Charles (brother), 22, 23, 24, 33, 52, 53, 54, 55, 56, 70
Norris, Frank (Benjamin Franklin, Jr.): attends Harvard, 20, 25; attends University of California, 20, 23-25; birth, 22; confusion of values, 146; death, 32; defends Dr. William Lawlor, 31; defends *Sister Carrie*, 30; greatness as a reporter, 70; life parallels that of Laura Jadwin in *The Pit*, 117; membership in Phi Gamma Delta, 19-21, 24; morality, 35, 43-44, 48; penchant for melodrama, 118, 127, 141; plans fictional trilogy about Battle of Gettysburg, 31; prissiness, 145; relations with father, 134-35; shyness about sex, 24, 113, 133; theory of education, 44-46; theory of fiction, 44-46; theory of masculine superiority, 85, 87-88; theory of nature, 102; visits Cuba, 28; visits Paris, 23; visits South Africa, 25-26

WRITINGS OF:

Blix (novel, 1899), 26, 27, 28, 44, 78-84, 87, 107-8, 134, 141, 142
"Boom" (short story, 1897), 122

"A Caged Lion" (short story, 1894), 52
"A Case for Lombroso" (short story, 1897), 40, 120
"Clothes of Steel" (article, 1889), 23
"A Deal in Wheat" (short story, 1902), 124-25, 140
A Deal in Wheat and Other Short Stories (1903), 122, 131
"A Defense of the Flag" (short story, 1895), 120
"The Dis-Associated Charities" (short story, 1897), 56, 121
"Dual Personality of Slick Dick Nickerson" (short story, 1902), 123
"Dying Fires" (short story, 1902), 31, 117, 124, 126, 134
"The End of the Act" (short story, 1895), 25, 120
"The End of the Beginning" (short story, 1897), 120
"Fantaisie Printaniere" (short story, 1897), 27, 119
"The Frontier Gone at Last" (essay, 1902), 39, 51
"The Great American Novel" (essay, 1903), 37
"His Dead Mother's Portrait" (short story, 1897), 121
"His Single Blessedness" (short story, 1897), 120, 122
"His Sister" (short story, 1896), 122
"The Jongleur of Taillebois" (short story, 1891), 50, 67
"Judy's Service of Gold Plate" (short story, 1897), 27, 119
"Lauth" (short story, 1893), 50, 51, 56
"Little Dramas of the Curbstone" (short story, 1897), 38, 121
"A Lost Story" (short story, 1903), 123
A Man's Woman (novel, 1900), 29, 50, 57, 84-87, 89, 101, 108, 116, 120, 139, 142
McTeague (novel, 1899), 21, 27, 28, 30, 32, 48, 53, 62-75, 76, 79,

104-5, 116, 117-18, 119, 120, 127, 130, 134, 136, 138, 139, 141, 142, 145

"The Mechanics of Fiction" (essay, 1901), 36

Moran of the Lady Letty (novel, 1898), 27, 28, 29, 32, 44, 76-78, 79, 87, 117, 130, 139, 142; (film, 1922), 32

"The National Spirit as It Relates to the Great American Novel" (essay, 1902), 40

"The Need for a Literary Conscience" (essay, 1901), 47

"A Neglected Epic" (essay, 1902), 104

"New York as a Literary Center" (essay, 1902), 36

"The Novel with a Purpose" (essay, 1902), 33, 37

The Octopus (novel, 1901), 21, 26, 30, 32, 35, 39-40, 43, 50, 62, 79, 89-106, 107, 116, 124, 127, 133-42 *passim*

"The Opinions of Leander" (sketches, 1897), 145, 146

"The Passing of Cock-Eye Blacklock" (short story, 1902), 31

The Pit (novel, 1903), 20, 21, 22, 25, 30, 32, 41, 48, 74, 86, 107-18, 123-27, 130, 131, 134, 135, 137, 140-42; (play, 1904, and film, 1917), 32

"A Plea for Romantic Fiction" (essay, 1901), 42

"A Problem in Fiction" (essay, 1901), 36, 37

"The Puppets and the Puppy" (dramatic sketch, 1897), 26, 121

The Responsibilities of the Novelist (collected essays, 1903), 33, 36-48

"The Riding of Felipe" (short story, 1901), 50, 125-26

"Salt and Sincerity" (essays, 1902), 43, 44

"Simplicity in Art" (essay, 1902), 36, 42, 45, 54

"Son of a Sheik" (short story, 1891), 51

"The Third Circle" (short story, 1897), 120, 122

The Third Circle (collected short stories, 1909), 119, 122

"Toppan" (short story, 1893), 52

"Travis Hallett's Half-Back" (short story, 1894), 51, 54

"True Reward of the Novelist" (essay, 1901), 37, 42-43, 101

"Two Hearts that Beat as One" (short story, 1903), 123

Vandover and the Brute (novel, 1914), 21, 22, 25, 30, 33, 44, 52-61, 62, 72, 73, 76, 79, 115, 116, 120, 124, 134, 137

"The Way of the World" (short story, 1892), 24

Yvernelle (poem, 1891), 24, 49-50, 52, 56, 125-26

Norris, Mrs. Gertrude Doggett (mother), 21, 23, 24, 25, 26, 29, 49, 135

Norris, Jeannette Black (wife), 26, 28, 29, 87

Norris, Jeannette, Jr. (daughter), 30, 33-34

Norris, Kathleen (sister-in-law), 33, 52

Norris, Lester (brother), 22, 23

North American Review, 127

O. Henry, 51

Old Poodle Dog Restaurant, 31

Oriental Exclusion Act, 120

Overland Monthly, 51

Parrington, Vernon, 128

Peixotto, Ernest, 23, 28

Peter Pan, 47, 60

Phi Gamma Delta, 19-21, 24, 26, 31, 33

Piper, Henry, 134

"Pit" (card game), 32

Pizer, Donald, 93-94, 133-34, 136-37, 142

Plagiarism, 31

Platonism, 37

Index

Poe, Edgar Allan, 133; "The Fall of the House of Usher," 120
Polk Street (San Francisco), 64, 66, 70, 72, 137
Pollock, Channing, 24, 32, 127
Pope, Alexander, 39, 143
Populist movement, 89-90
Porter, Bruce, 31
Pound, Ezra, 75
Presley (character in *The Octopus*), 44, 91, 92-96, 99, 134-35
Primitivism, 98, 138, 141

Reed, William T., 22
Reform movements, 38, 65, 89-90, 94, 140
Remington, Frederic, 28
Reninger, H. Willard, 90-92, 131
"Representational and Presentational" Art, 38
Republican Party, 89
Rhodes, Cecil, 25
Richards, Grant, 30
Riesman, David, 81
"Robber Barons," 50
"Robert d'Artois," 23
"Romantic anarchism," preface
Romanticism and Classicism, 143
Rome, 23
Rose, Guy, 23
Roselle, New Jersey, 29
Royle, Edwin Milton, 119

Sales figures of Norris' novels, 142
San Francisco Art Association, 23
San Francisco *Chronicle*, 23, 25
Santa Anita Ranch, 29
Saturday Evening Post, 32
Science and religion, conflict between, 60
Securities and Exchange Commission (SEC), 116
Self-indulgence, 52, 53, 56-57, 59, 86, 137
Shelgrim (character in *The Octopus*), 26, 91, 94-96, 99, 100, 106
Sherwood, John, 86
Sinclair, Upton, *The Jungle*, 89, 91
Smiles (University of California humor magazine), 24

Snell, George, *Shapers of American Fiction*, 132
Socrates, 141
Southern Agrarianism, 65
Southern Pacific Railroad, 26, 89, 94
Spanish-American War, 28
Stebbins, George C., 23
Steinbeck, John, 46; *The Grapes of Wrath*, 91, 99-100, 140, 144; "The Leader of the People," 82
Stevenson, Mr. and Mrs. Robert Louis, 31, 131
Stowe, Harriet Beecher, 37, 103, 143
Stroheim, Erich von, 33, 68, 142
"Sturgis, Justin" (Norris' pseudonym), 26
Subdivision "boom" of the 1890's, 122
Sunday-school art, 69

Taylor, Walter Fuller, *The Economic Novel in America*, 131
Telepathy, 93, 98
Television serials, 76
"Thing-handlers and symbol-handlers," 72-75, 78, 99, 144-45
Thoreau, Henry David, 38, 81, 97, 140
"Thoroughbreds," 77, 120-21
Three Friends (yacht), 28
Tompkins, Elizabeth, 46
Tompkins, Juliet Wilbor, 77, 86
Transcendentalism, preface, 36, 37, 38, 39, 91, 94, 137-38, 140
Truth, 36-37, 75
Turgenev, 132
Twain, Mark, 67, 128, 137

Underwood, John C., *Literature and Insurgency*, 128
University of California (Berkeley), 20, 23, 34, 44, 74

Valentino, Rudolph, 32
Vanamee (character in *The Octopus*), 44, 78, 90-92, 96-98, 102, 135, 138-39
Veblen, Thorstein, 22, 116
Verdi, 68

Wagner, 78; *Die Meistersinger,* 79

Walcutt, Charles C., *American Literary Naturalism,* 32, 103, 109, 131, 136

Walker, Franklin, *Frank Norris* (biography), 31, 46, 129-30; *Letters of Frank Norris,* 136-37

Washington Square, 29

Waterhouse, Seymour, 27

Wave (San Francisco), 26, 27, 31, 46, 48, 76, 101, 119

Wharton, Edith, 130

Whitman, Walt, 142; "Nay, Tell Me Not To-day the Publish'd Shame," 38; "Song of the Redwood Tree," 137

Women's suffrage movement, 87-88

Wordsworth, William, 47

Works Progress Administration (WPA), 131

World's Work, 36

Yale University, 76, 142

Zola, Émile, 23, 24, 25, 30, 31, 52, 56, 127, 131, 132

DATE DUE
